THE PATTERN
of
GOD'S TRUTH

Problems of Integration in
Christian Education

By

FRANK E. GAEBELEIN

BMH Books
P.O. Box 544
Winona Lake, Indiana 46590
bmhbooks.com

THE PATTERN OF GOD'S TRUTH

CONTENTS

CONTENTS

PREFACE TO THE PAPERBACK EDITION

Of my writings on education, this book discusses what I still believe, fourteen years after its first publication, to be the master principle of all education, Christian or secular. That all truth is of God is certainly no new concept. Its roots are biblical, and it has been expressed since apostolic times by men of the caliber of Augustine, Melanchthon, Pascal, Newman and Kuyper. Yet in more recent years the far-reaching implications of the unity of all truth in God have too often been overlooked. One of the continuing needs of our time is the reassertion of the fact that all truth is of God, that Christ is the incarnate Word of truth, that the Holy Spirit is the Spirit of truth, and that Scripture is the written Word of truth. Along with this reassertion there should come a fuller realization that both the natural creation and the creative endeavors of man in all fields are in all their aspects related to God's truth. For a dichotomy between sacred and secular truth has no place in a consistently Christian philosophy of education.

While I might now express differently certain things set forth in these lectures, the differences would not be major. I am more firmly convinced than ever that to be genuinely Christian a liberal education must be based upon the unity of truth in God. The commitment of an increasing number of Christian schools and colleges to the thoroughgoing practice of this principle seems to me an evidence that what Kendig Brubaker Cully calls in the title of a recent book "The Search for a Christian Education" is proceeding on the right path.

Let me express appreciation to Mr. Wilbur D. Ruggles and Mr. Walter T. Oakley of Oxford University Press for granting permission for the publication of *The Pattern of God's Truth* in paperback. And to Moody Press I am particularly grateful for their readiness to undertake this project, thereby making the book available to a wider readership.

FRANK E. GAEBELEIN

Arlington, Virginia
March 1968

PREFACE

This book is in the nature of a supplement to the author's *Christian Education in a Democracy*. The larger volume, which appeared in 1951 as the Report of the N.A.E. Committee on The Philosophy and Practice of Christian Education, covered education from elementary school through college and of necessity alluded only briefly to some matters of vital importance. Therefore, the invitation to deliver the Griffith Thomas Memorial Lectures for 1952 at Dallas Theological Seminary and to discuss Christian education was particularly welcome. The following chapters comprise these lectures. They were repeated at the Conservative Baptist Theological Seminary of Denver as the Lectures on Christian Thought and Ministry for the fall of 1953.

At the heart of all thinking about education, whether Christian or secular, lies the problem of integration. Education is a living thing; no less than the individual it must have a philosophy. In general, education in America rests upon definite presuppositions. But it by no means follows that because a philosophy of education has been adopted it is being consistently put into practice. To declare allegiance to an educational point of view is one thing; to integrate a school or college in all its parts—curriculum, student activities, administration, and everything else—with that point of view is another thing.

It is at this point that much of Christian as well as secular education is inadequate. Committed to high doctrine and a view of the world based upon Biblical truth, a good part of Christian education falls short of bringing all of its practice into living relation with this truth. Its principles may be lofty and of unexceptionable orthodoxy, but in practice of these principles it has far to go.

The following chapters have been written by an evangelical Christian who has education of this theological persuasion as his primary consideration. Yet the subject discussed is bigger than any particular aspect of Christian thought. Therefore, it may well be that those whose theological views are different from the author's may find these pages of interest and help in their endeavor to achieve a living union between Christianity and education.

Frank E. Gaebelein

Stony Brook, New York
February 1954

ACKNOWLEDGMENTS

To President John F. Walvoord and the faculty of Dallas Theological Seminary I am grateful for the invitation that led to the writing of these lectures. I am indebted also to President Carey S. Thomas and the faculty of the Conservative Baptist Theological Seminary of Denver for the opportunity of delivering them a second time, an experience that resulted in the clarification of certain points. The Oxford University Press has given me both encouragement and advice, and for this too I am grateful.

Appreciation is due the following who have generously granted permission to use published material:

The Christian Century for quotations from the issues of 10 September 1952 and 25 February 1953;

Wm. B. Eerdmans Publishing Company for a quotation from *A Christian Philosophy of Education* by Gordon Clark;

The Inter-Varsity Christian Fellowship for a quotation from the May 1952 issue of *His;*

John Murray of London for a quotation from *The House of Quiet* by A. C. Benson;

The National Preparatory School Committee

for a quotation from the April 1949 issue of *Information Service;*

The Naylor Company for a quotation from *Christianity and American Education* by Edwin H. Rian;

The Princeton University Press for a quotation from *Poetry as a Means of Grace* by Charles Grosvenor Osgood;

The Westminister Press for a quotation from *The Great Shorter Works of Pascal,* translated by Emile Cailliet and John C. Blankenagel.

CHAPTER ONE

INTEGRATION AND THE TRUTH

'Sanctify them through the truth: thy word is truth.'
John 17:17

1. *By Way of Introduction*

ONE April morning early in the first century, a Roman procurator said three words that have echoed through the ages. As the Man Christ Jesus stood before him, Pontius Pilate asked, 'What is truth?' Sir Francis Bacon notwithstanding, the words were far from a jest. No one faced with Pilate's responsibility of passing judgment upon the Man who had just looked him in the eye and said, 'To this end was I born, and for this cause came I into the world, that I should bear witness unto the truth,' [1] could be in a laughing mood. Sophisticated, certainly; skeptical, undoubtedly; but not joking.

There was nothing original about the procurator's question; for centuries the sages and philosophers had been asking it. Nor was there anything final about it; ever since that day in Jerusalem it has, in one form or another, been in the minds and on the lips of philosophers, scientists, artists, poets, teachers, and thoughtful

3

men of every sort. It is the age-old query, the perennial question of the human spirit.

In the lectures before us we are to deal with the answer to that question in relation to one of the chief responsibilities committed to the Christian church — the responsibility for education, the nurture and training of youth in the truth of God and in that fear of the Lord which is the beginning of wisdom. You will understand me, then, when I say that the preparation of these pages has been accompanied by a special sense of obligation. More than that, it has brought with it a burden of humility. Even thirty years spent by one man in a corner of the vast field of Christian education, so much of which needs still to be explored, do not justify an attitude savoring in any way of the oracular. As James Stalker of Aberdeen said in beginning a series of addresses on preaching, 'It is with no sense of having attained that I am to speak to you; for I always seem to myself to be beginning to learn my trade . . .' [2]

At the same time, I should affirm that what I have to say expresses personal conviction. For there are some things of which Christians are sure. These things are the great verities of the faith. Christianity is a revealed religion, not a human invention. Therefore, convictions respecting it are initially based on faith. Yet there is a sense in which the convictions of faith become more fully our own, as we practice and learn them in the laboratory of daily life and work. It is out of such convictions, first believed and then matured by experience of what happens in the field of education when God's truth is either honored or ignored, as the case may be, that these lectures have grown.

2. *The Relevance of the Subject*

The Pattern of God's Truth: Problems of Integration in Christian Education. Perhaps some are wondering what a subject like this has to do with seminary students and faculty or, for that matter, with the general Christian reader. 'Must every minister or missionary, theological student or professor,' the question is asked, 'really be concerned with Christian education? Even more, should all Christians be interested in it?' The Bible answers 'Yes.' For it takes only a glance at the hundreds of listings of such words as 'child' and 'children' that are to be found in a concordance to demonstrate the fact that the Bible has a great deal to say about youth. Some day a thoughtful student of Christian education will make a thorough study of every reference in the Bible to children and will go on to develop inductively the principles of child training set forth in the Word of God. The result of such an investigation may turn out to be a major contribution to Christian thought.

For the present, however, we need look no farther than the fourth chapter of Ephesians to be assured of the relevance of our subject. St. Paul, who has been enumerating the gifts of Christ, mentions in the eleventh verse, 'pastors and teachers.' * It is evident from the Greek text, says Dean Alford, that in this case the two offices were held by the same persons.[3] In short, while apostles, prophets, and evangelists are listed separately, 'pastors and teachers' belong together grammatically and also logically.

There is nothing arbitrary about this. Whatever else a pastor does, he deals in some way with youth. There are children in all congregations, if not in every home. Churches have Sunday Schools. Young people from churches go to school, and their attitudes and response to their ministers reflect something of the teaching they are receiving. In missionary work, teaching goes hand in hand with evangelizing. And beyond all this is the fact that both home and community are constantly exercising an informal though often decisive influence upon youth. Among the most effective of all teachers are fathers and moth-

---

* 'And he gave some, apostles; and some, prophets; and some, evangelists; and some, pastors and teachers.'

ers, brothers, sisters, and friends. In short, teaching, in one form or another, is always going on
and is as inescapable as life itself. One of the com-
monest misconceptions of education is that which
limits it to the four walls of the schoolroom or, to
broaden the figure, to the acreage of the campus.
In reality, however, education is a continuing
process as broad as experience itself, and one in
which all who have contact with youth share,
either consciously or unconsciously. Therefore,
it follows that a ministry not interested in education is only half a ministry, and that we who are
called to be ambassadors for Christ cannot but
be deeply concerned with something so vitally
linked to our cause as Christian education.

3. The Problem of Integration

From this brief view of the relevance of our
subject, we turn to its analysis. At first glance,
there seem to be two separate things before us:
'God's truth' and the matter of 'integration.' In
reality, however, the two are closely linked. God's
truth is of universal scope. This being the case,
every aspect of education must be brought into
relation to it. So the problem of integration arises
— the word, we are reminded, means 'the bringing together of parts into the whole.' Our aim
will be to point the way to a solution of this prob-

lem by showing how in some vital particulars Christian education can achieve integration into the all-embracing truth of God.

It was Josiah Royce who said that every idea has both internal meaning and external meaning.[4] The principle may be applied to Christian education. Using 'external' not in its connotation of 'superficial' but rather in its denotation of something outside and beyond us, we see that the external meaning of Christian education has to do with God's truth. That is to say, it is objectively true. Whether or not we know it or understand it, believe it, or teach it, it remains His truth. And as we come to knowledge of it, we find that it is nothing less than the context of everything that we know or ever can know. In the words of John Henry Newman, 'Religious truth is not only a portion but a condition of general knowledge.' [5] As for the internal meaning of Christian education, it is something quite different. It relates to the inner workings of education, to all of its courses and every one of its policies. And in addition it also has to do with the integration of these things with its external meaning.

The latter statement leads to an important qualification. On the one hand, God's truth is external to Christian education in that it is not dependent upon what education is or does. On the other hand, there is, as integration proceeds, a merging of the internal into the external. Thus the internal, though always subordinate to the external, joins in living union with the external, which remains transcendently beyond it. This is the heart of integration and the crux of the matter.

At this point, an analogy will help us. Consider astronomy. It has to do not just with the solar system but also with the whole vast stellar universe, pointing, as does all creation, to the eternal power and Godhead of Him who made all things. This is its external meaning, its context. But then there is the astronomer, discovering step by step from the vantage point of this little earth one truth after another relating to the well-nigh infinite context of his science. As he follows the principles and techniques of astronomy and as he uses them to think truly about astronomy — that is, in accordance with the external reality of the universe — what he discovers takes its place as part of the spacious external realm to which it belongs.

So with integration in Christian education. It is the living union of its subject matter, administration, and even of its personnel, with the eternal and infinite pattern of God's truth. This, as we have already said, is the heart of integration and the crux of the problem.

For problem it is; let us make no mistake about

that. In fact, it is not the slightest exaggeration to say that this matter of integration, or uniting the parts into a living whole, is the problem of problems, not only in Christian education but also in all other education as well. Behind every perplexity, difficulty, and dilemma with which our schools and colleges are faced is this central one: How to achieve this unity? How to put together the diverse fragments that make up the raw material of education? These are questions that are being asked by secular educators with the insistence of those who have let go their moorings and are drifting upon uncharted seas. 'There is nothing,' says Professor Kandel of Columbia, 'that so clearly illustrates the uncertainty and instability of American education as the perennial addiction to defining its aims, objectives, and goals' [6]; and Dr. Scott Buchanan makes this frank admission: 'We do not know what we ought to learn in education. We have not been able to discern the pattern in our knowledges which would make them one knowledge.' [7] Or, as the authors of the Harvard Report on *General Education in a Free Society* declare, 'the search continues and must continue for some over-all logic, some strong, not easily broken frame within which both college and school may fulfill their at once diversifying and uniting task.' [8]

And so it must. An education that has deliberately departed from God and His Word will continue to search, 'ever learning and never able to come to knowledge of the truth,' to use Paul's words to Timothy.[9] This is why secular education today, including much of our public-school system, is still centrifugal, despite the vain efforts being made to base it on values derived solely from a sociological and naturalistic setting. Having turned its back upon God and His Word and having thus given up its external meaning, secular education is powerless to put together its internal meaning.

Christian education is different. With all its inadequacies, failures, and difficulties, it has something to which to tie itself. For it, too, integration is a problem, but a problem of quite another kind than for secular education. Christian education does not need to keep looking for the integrating factor; it already has this factor. We who believe the Bible to be the inspired Word of God and who take seriously such truths as the creation of the universe by the living God, the lost condition of man, the atonement, justification by faith, the reality of the resurrection, and the fellowship of believers in the Church know the answer to the secularist's vain search. The problem with which these lectures have to do, therefore, is not so much one of discovery as it is one of application.

At this point, we who are committed to the Christian view of education need to examine our hearts, lest there be anything of pride within us. If for us the unifying factor is the historic faith revealed in Scripture, we can only be very humble about it. Only by the grace of God are we what we are. There is nothing new, and certainly nothing original, in our position, for the faith which we hold has in the past served as the frame of reference for American education. It takes but a glance at the history of our oldest colleges and schools to show that they were founded, without exception, upon the Biblical position and that this position was for them a most practical and vivifying principle. For example, Harvard was founded in 1636 for training the Gospel ministry; its charter of 1650 said that the university had been established 'to educate the English and Indian youth in knowledge and godliness,' and it had for its motto *Christo et Ecclesiae*. Sixty-five years later, Yale was founded by those who feared Harvard was becoming unorthodox. The purpose of Columbia, begun in 1754, was 'to engage the children to know God in Jesus Christ.' But the roll could be called of William and Mary, Princeton, Dartmouth, Rutgers, along with other of our older colleges, and similar religious purposes would be revealed. So also with the denominational colleges and especially the women's col-

leges like Vassar, Smith, Wellesley, and Mt.
Holyoke.

Let us remember these things, lest in some
lapse into boasting we say of ourselves: 'We are
the people. We alone have a corner upon truth.
We only of all men have discovered the unifying
factor of education.' No, we have done nothing
of the kind. The most we can claim is that we
have recovered it, and this by the grace of God.
But why claim anything for ourselves? It is
enough that Christian education today has the
one principle that can give learning a frame of
reference spacious enough to comprehend all
knowledge and dynamic enough to develop
moral and spiritual maturity in the midst of a
materialistic and violent age.

4. *A Venture in Self-criticism*

Does this mean, then, that we have all the answers? On the contrary, it means nothing of the
kind. Granted that we have returned to the only
true unifying principle, there remains for us the
whole broad realm of application. So our problems multiply. And 'problems' mean knots to be
untied, needs to be met, errors to be corrected.
They point to unrealized aims, and at the same
time look toward solutions.

But though we shall be occupied with some
of the hard places in Christian education, the

achievements of those schools and colleges committed to the Gospel and to the Word of God
must not be forgotten. These achievements are
already large and make up an impressive chapter
in the history of American education. Among
them are such things as the remarkable growth of
Christian schools and colleges in America in the
last thirty years, the rise of the Christian day-
school movement, the coming of age education-
ally of the Bible institute and Bible college, the
foundation and growth of new theological seminaries, the revitalization in many places of the
Sunday School, and the development of addi-
tional agencies of Christian education, such as the
Daily Vacation Bible School, Child Evangelism,
Young Life Campaign, and the Inter-Varsity
Christian Fellowship.

We are not concerned, however, with ex-
pounding that chapter. On the contrary, the
choice of the subject before us has grown out of
the conviction that, great as the achievements of
evangelical Christian education have been, there
is much ground to be occupied and some serious
error, in both practice and theory, to be corrected. In other words, we are embarking on a
venture in constructive thinking, coupled with
self-criticism.

That self-criticism is necessary is evident. The
time has come, after decades of growth upon the

part of Christian education — growth which continues unabated — for us to have the maturity to look within; to measure ourselves by the criteria of truth set forth in the Word of God and apprehended through other sources as well; and, having thus seen some of our problems, to work bravely and honestly toward their solution. Like Paul the Apostle, Christian education, while it gives thanks for realized achievement, must say of itself: 'Not as though I had already attained, either were already perfect . . . I count not myself to have apprehended . . . I press toward the mark for the prize of the high calling of God in Christ Jesus.' [10]

Let us face the fact. When it comes to the application of the noble principles upon which it is built, Christian education in America has much to learn. We have had a great deal to say about God-centered, Christ-oriented, Bible-based education. But in actual practice we are not doing nearly enough of it. The old Negro spiritual, 'Everybody talkin' 'bout heav'n ain't goin' there,' might be paraphrased somewhat as follows: 'Everybody talkin' 'bout Christian education ain't doin' it.' This is not to say, of course, that we are not to any extent practicing Christian education. That is too extreme a judgment. Nevertheless, in respect to a thorough-going integration of Christ and the Bible with the whole institution, with all departments of study, with all kinds of student activities, with all phases of administration, there remains much land to be taken.

The trouble is that a good many Christian institutions are unconsciously deceiving themselves. Not even the theological seminary is exempt from criticism at this point. For it is a fact that in many a seminary the Bible has what amounts to a secondary place; though the program contains plenty of courses about the Bible — its criticism, interpretation, and languages — the student learns too little of the Word of God itself in its plain and forthright power. Therefore, it is entirely possible for students to go to some seminaries and come out knowing much about higher criticism, dialectic theology, the philosophy of religion, sociology, worship programs, and the like, and yet have only a bowing acquaintance with great portions of Scripture. As for many evangelical schools and colleges, because they have daily chapel services, Bible departments, and flourishing student activities of a Christian nature, they conclude that they are Christ-centered, Bible-based institutions, when in reality they have not yet grown up to that stature. There is no originality in the latter judgment. Others have been clear-sighted in recognizing the fact.

For example, Professor Gordon Clark of But-
ler University speaks of the Christian college,
where such good things as 'giving out tracts . . .
holding fervent prayer meetings, going out on
gospel teams, opening classes with prayer' are the
accepted practice; 'yet the actual instruction is
no more Christian than in a respectable secular
school . . . The program is merely a pagan education with a chocolate covering of Christianity.
And the pill, not the coating, works . . . the students are deceived into thinking that they have
received a Christian education when as a matter
of fact their training has been neither Christian
nor an education . . . Christianity, far from being a Bible-department religion, has a right to
control the instruction in all departments. The
general principles of Scripture apply to all subjects, and in some subjects the Scriptures supply
rather detailed principles, so that every course of
instruction is altered by a conscious adoption of
Christian principles.' [11]

These are plain words and perhaps some con-
cession should be made for the fact that their
writer may have overdrawn the picture. Yet the
fact that the situation described exists to some
degree cannot be blinked.

Dr. Edwin H. Rian puts it somewhat more
temperately but at the same time incisively. 'A
Christian theory of education,' he writes, 'is an

exposition of the idea that Christianity is a world and life view and not simply a series of unrelated doctrines. Christianity includes all of life. Every realm of knowledge, every aspect of life and every fact of the universe find their place and their answer within Christianity. It is a system of truth enveloping the entire world in its grasp . . . The present tendency in education to add religion to the courses of study is comparable to attaching a garage to a home. What the building of knowledge needs is not a new garage but a new foundation . . .' [12]

It is well for us to realize that there are still others who share this view. While both Professor Clark and Dr. Rian are evangelicals, there are other groups who recognize the challenge of an all-embracing religious frame of reference. Important work, for instance, has been done in this field through the Hazen Foundation, the publications of which, though written from a liberal point of view theologically, show a deep concern for the integration of religion with the various departments of learning. To be sure, the integration is in this case rather with liberalism than with the distinctive positions of supernatural Christianity. The fact remains that a serious approach to the problem is being made and a reasoned presentation of a definite point of view is being published, something still to be done on

any comparable scale by evangelicals. The acknowledgment of these things is, then, a needed
corrective to the provincialism into which we,
in our zeal for our view, sometimes lapse. Nor
does this acknowledgment dull the edge of our
faith or compromise in any way our conviction
that in the great doctrines of Scripture we have
the true integrating factor of Christian education. It is simply an incentive for us to set to work
and apply to every aspect of our schools the comprehensive pattern of God's truth.

5. God's Truth and Its Implications

The time has now come to step aside from the
near view of the problem and see the direction in
which we are going. Reflection upon the nature
of our unifying principle will light up our road.
To say that we hold Christ and the Bible as central to education demands that we do some hard
thinking about God's truth, which is the over-all
context of our problem.

For one thing, it leads us into a consideration
of truth and its nature. None of us will deny to
Christ a personal identification with truth. Pilate's question, 'What is truth?' had already been
answered in the upper room when our Lord said,
'I am the way, the truth, and the life.' [13] But
Christ's identification with truth does not depend only on that affirmation; it rests rather on

every word He spoke and every act He performed. The reason those three brief years He spent in teaching men, ministering to their needs, and finally dying for them outweigh in influence all the writings of all the philosophers is that in Him men saw once and for all the truth. And if Christ Himself is truth incarnate, let us not forget that He also identified truth with the Scriptures, when He prayed to His Father in behalf of His own, 'Sanctify them through the truth: Thy word is truth.' [14] This was no theoretical statement. On the contrary, our Lord's habitual use of Scripture leaves no doubt of the fact that for Him the written Word was truth indeed.

To Christian orthodoxy these facts are elementary. But their broad implications are not so obvious. Truth, though it comprehends finite things, is greater than all it comprehends; its only limitation is the acceptance of its opposite, which is error. And though it includes the finite, it has also its infinite dimensions, because it inheres in the very nature of God Himself. For Christian education, therefore, to adopt as its unifying principle Christ and the Bible means nothing short of the recognition that *all truth is God's truth*. It is no accident that St. Paul, setting before the Philippian church a charter for Christian thought, wrote: 'Finally, brethren, whatsoever things are true* . . . think on these things.' [15] He knew that Christian truth embraces all truth, and that nothing true is outside the scope of Christianity.

Now the next step is where many have faltered. In all candor it must be admitted that much education called Christian has failed to see that this comprehensive fact of all truth being God's truth breaks down, on the one hand, the division of knowledge between secular and religious; and brings, on the other hand, every area of life and thought 'into captivity to the obedience of Christ,' [16] to use the great Pauline phrase. To put it bluntly, we have been too prone to set up a false dichotomy in our thinking and thus in our education. We have rightly enthroned the Word of God as the ultimate criterion of truth; we have rightly given pre-eminence to the Lord Jesus Christ as the incarnation of the God of all truth. But at the same time we have fallen into the error of failing to see as clearly as we should that there are areas of truth not fully explicated in Scripture and that these, too, are part of God's truth. Thus we have made the misleading distinction between sacred and secular, forgetting that, as Cervantes said in one of those flashes of

* The word 'true' is here the first of a series — 'honest,' 'just,' 'pure,' 'lovely,' 'of good report' — each member of which may be thought of as an aspect of the truth.

wisdom that punctuate the strange doings of Don Quixote, 'Where the truth is, in so far as it is truth, there God is.' [17]

We are now at a place where we must think with particular care. We must do this because lack of clarity at this point may lead to the charge of elevating truth in relation to mundane things to an equality with revealed truth. As a matter of fact, however, such a conclusion does not necessarily follow from the premise that all truth is God's truth. It is perfectly possible to recognize the diverse importance of different aspects of truth without in any way denying its indissoluble nature. We do indeed give the primacy to that spiritual truth revealed in the Bible and incarnate in Christ. That does not mean, however, that those aspects of truth discoverable by man in the realm of mathematics, chemistry, or geography, are any whit less God's truth than the truth as it is in Christ. The difference is clearly a question of subject matter. In the latter case, the subject matter is of a different importance from the former; truth about Christ pertains to salvation, that about physics does not. To be sincerely mistaken regarding scientific truth is one thing; to be mistaken, even sincerely, regarding such truth as the Person and the work of the Lord Jesus Christ is another thing. But all the time there is the unity of all truth under God, and that unity we deny in education at the peril of habituating ourselves to the fragmentary kind of learning found on some avowedly Christian campuses today.

The call, then, is for a wholly Christian world view on the part of our education. We must recognize, for example, that we need teachers who see their subjects, whether scientific, historical, mathematical, literary, or artistic, as included within the pattern of God's truth. It is one thing to take for ourselves the premise that all truth is God's truth. It is another thing to build upon this premise an effective educational practice that shows the student the unity of truth and that brings alive in his heart and mind the grand concept of a Christ who 'is the image of the invisible God,' by whom 'all things were created,' who 'is before all things,' and by whom 'all things consist,' [18] or hold together.

If this is our position, if we actually mean to stand upon this ground, then we are driven to some searching conclusions. Let us not hesitate to state them simply and directly, leaving our conscience to make whatever application is needed. Once more, then, we set down the premise: All truth is God's truth. Whereupon we must conclude that Christian education has a holy obligation to stand for and honor the truth wherever it is found. With Justin Martyr, we must declare: 'All that has been well said belongs to us Christians.' [19] To be sure, revealed truth, as stated in the Word of God and known through Christ, is of higher importance than natural truth. But the latter is also within the pattern of God's truth. Thus it follows that for any of us, orthodox though our beliefs may be, to try to support revealed truth either by denying any other aspect of truth or by suppressing or distorting it is an offense against the very nature of God, as well as a lapse into the immoral doctrine that the end justifies the means.

What has just been said is especially relevant to preaching. Every preacher of the Bible ought constantly to ask himself questions like this: 'Is my exegesis true?' 'Is this sermon of mine, no matter how clever and effective, really presenting what Scripture actually says?' Many an attractive and highly praised sermon is based on an irresponsible exegesis. And who has not heard some time-worn illustration told from the pulpit not only as true but as a personal experience of the preacher, when it is nothing of the kind? When it comes to the matter of a responsible handling of the Word of God, John Calvin, the prince of expositors, set a standard that all who preach might well emulate. 'I have not to my knowledge,' he said, 'corrupted or twisted a single passage . . .

and when I could have drawn out a far-fetched meaning, if I had studied subtlety, I had put the temptation under foot.' [20]

But the logic of the sacredness of the truth is a two-edged sword that cuts both ways. Therefore we must say in faithful warning to those of a theologically liberal persuasion that for them to suppress or distort any aspect of the truth revealed in the Word of God and incarnate in the Person of Christ, in order to support natural truth, is equally an offense against the God of all truth and a lapse into justifying the means by the end.

The solemn fact is that truth is holy; inherent in the nature of God Himself, it is ever sacred. No man who tampers with it is guiltless. The Bible closes with an unmistakable emphasis upon truth. When John on Patmos sees heaven open, he identifies the returning King by the Name, 'Faithful and True.' [21] And when he describes the New Jerusalem, he reminds us that there will be no place in it for any violation of the truth, because 'there shall in no wise enter into it anything . . . that maketh a lie.' [22] Let us remember that God makes no mistakes in emphasis; as we go on to struggle with some hard problems, let us do so with a zealous regard for the truth, realizing in deep humility that we may indeed fail to apprehend it in all its sacred perfection, but trusting also that the God of all truth will show us the way to His greater glory in our Christian education.

Notes

1. John 18:37.
2. *The Preacher and His Models*, by James Stalker, London, 1891, p. 3.
3. *The Greek Testament*, by Henry Alford, Boston, 1878, vol. III, p. 117.
4. Cited in *The Christian Approach to Culture*, by Emile Cailliet, New York, 1953, p. 32.
5. *The Idea of a University*, by John Henry Cardinal Newman, London, 1901, p. 70.
6. *Goals for American Education*, New York, 1950, p. 508.
7. Ibid. p. 143.
8. *General Education in a Free Society*, Cambridge, 1945, p. 40.
9. II Timothy 3:7.
10. Philippians 3:12–14.
11. *A Christian Philosophy of Education*, Grand Rapids, pp. 208–10. Used by permission.
12. *Christianity and American Education*, by Edwin H. Rian, San Antonio, 1949, p. 236. Used by permission.
13. John 14:6.
14. John 17:17.
15. Philippians 4:8.
16. II Corinthians 10:5.
17. *The Adventures of Don Quixote*, by Miguel de Cervantes Saavedra, translated by J. M. Cohen, Middlesex, 1950, p. 490.
18. Colossians 1:15–17.
19. Justin Martyr, *Second Apology*, p. 13, quoted by Cailliet, op. cit. p. 62.

20. Quoted by Georgia Harkness, *John Calvin: The Man and His Ethics*, New York, 1931, p. 259.
21. Revelation 19:11.
22. Revelation 22:15.

CHAPTER TWO

THE TEACHER AND THE TRUTH

'Be not conformed to this world: but be you
transformed by the renewing of your mind.'
Romans 12:2

1. *Determining the Truth*

OUR discussion thus far has led to the premise
that all truth is God's truth. Not only so; it has
identified as the unifying factor of Christian education the Bible with its life-giving revelation
of Christ. Now we must travel farther along this
road. As we begin to do so, some questions arise:
'What is the criterion of this all-enveloping
truth? Tell us, if you will, how to distinguish the
true from the false.' In some such words the challenge comes.

And it is a fair one, not honestly to be evaded.
Looking again at Cervantes' words: 'Where' the
truth is, in so far as it is the truth, there God is,' [1]
we see that it is with the conditional clause, 'in so
far as it is the truth,' that we are at present concerned. How to determine the truth — as Ham-
let said, 'there's the rub.'

There are three approaches to this matter:
from the point of view of revelation alone, from

the point of view of revelation plus reason, and from the point of view of reason only. We have already gone far enough to have made a choice: ours is the approach by way of revelation plus reason. To make revelation the only means of knowing what is true or false in every field may lead to irrationalism with the danger of decrying the God-given faculty of reason. This is not for a moment to deny that God's truth has been revealed: rather a recognition of the fact that in apprehending and in discovering new aspects of it, our reason plays, under the guidance of the Spirit of God, a necessary part. At the opposite pole is the view that makes human reason alone the means of knowing truth. This we must unequivocally reject, because it by-passes God's revelation and ends up in rationalism and humanism, making the mind of the natural man the measure of all things.

For the Christian, then, the seat of truth is God's revelation, contained primarily in the inspired Word but manifest also in creation. And this truth, though on its highest level received by faith, can also be known through our reason, enlightened by the Holy Spirit. The preceding sentence expands the idea of truth held by some Christians. It brings to our attention another sphere of God's revelation — that of nature. When we say that God has two books, we are on solid scriptural ground. There is, for example, the Nineteenth Psalm, the first six verses of which tell us that the heavens, the firmament, day and night, and the very sun itself unite in their witness to the glory of God and the greatness of His handiwork, while the remainder of the psalm pays tribute to the written Word. Even more plainly, the opening argument of Paul's indictment in Romans of human sin is that, having the witness of God in nature—that is to say, having God's book of creation open before him and being able to read in it the divine power and Godhead — man is inexcusable, because, neither recognizing nor glorifying God, he has followed his own foolish and darkened heart.*

Any adequate basis for Christian education must, therefore, include God's revelation in creation as well as in His written Word. But our human understanding of the book of nature must not be made the norm for acceptance of the other book, the Bible. To the contrary, Christian education must recognize the fragmentary state of our knowledge of the vast book of the created

* 'The invisible things of him from the creation of the world are clearly seen, being understood by the things that are made, even his eternal power and Godhead; so that they are without excuse; because that when they knew God, they glorified him not as God, neither were thankful, but became vain in their imaginations and their foolish heart was darkened.' 2

universe. The attitude of an Einstein, who compares the universe to a watch, the case of which is forever locked, and likens the scientist to a man who, from the outside, must find out its intricate workings, holds a lesson for us. A great deal of humility is needed to avoid the rash assurance with which some Christians who know next to nothing about the spacious realm of science dogmatize regarding the book of creation.

All the time, however, the ultimate criterion of truth is found in the revealed Word, the Bible. This is not to say that Christians know everything there is to know about the meaning of that criterion. It is still true, and always will be, until the time of the new heavens and new earth, that we 'see through a glass darkly.' Nevertheless, we of an age far removed from that of St. Paul should be able to profit by the lessons of the past. We should remember that there was a day when Ptolemaic astronomy was equated with Scripture truth. The equation was wrong, as even the strictest fundamentalist now knows; it was not Scripture that was faulty, but the Christian understanding of Scripture. So also when the church finally admitted the truth of Copernican astronomy, the Bible was illuminated, not overthrown.

In our day, the same principle holds; it is becoming increasingly plain, for example, that man is far older than the traditional 6,000 years. The newest development that is shedding light on his antiquity is the carbon clock. Its discovery is a fascinating page in contemporary science. Study of the cosmic rays pouring in upon us from outer space led to an understanding of the nuclear process taking place in the upper atmosphere. This study showed that cosmic rays produce neutrons which turn the atmospheric nitrogen into radioactive carbon. At the same time, ordinary carbon is also present in the air, and both kinds of carbon, radioactive and ordinary, join with oxygen to make carbon dioxide. Moreover, carbon dioxide, whether radioactive or normal — it makes no difference — is absorbed by plants and by animals that eat plants.

It was Dr. Willard F. Libby, of the Institute for Nuclear Studies at the University of Chicago, who first ascertained the exact proportion of radioactive carbon to ordinary carbon in the air. And from this clue the strange clock was developed. For it was known that radioactive carbon atoms, just like all radioactive atoms, decay at a constant average rate. Thus after 5,568 years only about one-half the original amount of radioactive carbon atoms will be left. Another 5,568 years will dissipate one-half of the residue, and the process will go on until in 25,000 years only one-thirtieth of the original amount will remain. Beyond 30,000 years, measurement is impossible with present techniques because the concentration of radioactive carbon atoms is so minute.

Now it is a fact that all living animals and plants contain these two kinds of carbon in the same proportion as they are in the air. But immediately upon death, the intake of carbon stops. Then the clock begins running, measuring the years by disintegration of the radioactive carbon. So it is that the specialist can take a charred stick or bone — provided that it is less than approximately 30,000 years old — count the radioactive carbon with a Geiger tube, and thus calculate the age.

Here are a few findings in relation to man. Woven sandals buried in Fort Rock Cave near Crater Lake, Oregon, have been dated at some 9,000 years ago. Burned bone of an extinct species of bison with spear points made by man, found at Tepexepan, Mexico, and Clovis, New Mexico, have been shown to be 10,000 years old. One of the leaders in this field, Professor J. Laurence Kulp of the Geology Department at Columbia University, told the writer that artifacts from a cave in France have been given an age of 14,000 years by the carbon clock.

And so it goes. Clearly the traditional ideas of the antiquity of man will have to be revised. But will this change the essential truth of the wonderful Genesis account of creation? Certainly not; on the contrary, it will simply broaden and deepen our understanding of that truth.[3]

Such things as these raise questions of interpretation — important, to be sure, yet still interpretation. Behind them lie certain truths that are plainly written in the Bible for all men to see and believe. It is these that make up the framework of our Christian world view. What are they? They are the facts upon which Christianity rests. Included in them are the existence of the living God, the Maker of heaven and earth; man's creation in the image of God, an image ruined through the fall beyond human power to repair, but not beyond God's power to regenerate; the incarnation of God the Son and His redemption of lost humanity; the activity of God the Holy Spirit in calling out of this present world a community of believers which is Christ's Body, the Church; and, finally, the end of earthly history through the 'glorious appearing of the great God and our Saviour Jesus Christ.' [4]

Let us understand once and for all that there is nothing sectarian about these truths; they are common to all branches of the Christian church. Granted that in many quarters they have been and are today being watered down through concessions and reservations, or obscured through man-made tradition and dogma, the fact remains that such truths as these stand as both the foundation and frame of reference for a Christian world view. It is upon them that Christian education must build; it is within them that it must work.

2. No Christian Education without Christian Teachers

We are now ready for an important conclusion. It is this: The moment a person takes the position that all truth is God's truth, he is committed to doing something. The Bible knows no such thing as truth that is merely theoretical; in the Bible the truth is linked to the deed. We see this principle in its highest expression in the atonement. As theory alone, the atonement, profoundly true though it is, could never save a single soul. For the atonement to have saving efficacy, He who is the truth had to 'do' it in His redemptive work on Calvary. Likewise with the whole of Scripture truth; it must be related to life to be known for what it really is. So it follows that for Christian education to adopt the principle that all truth is God's truth means not only words but also deeds.

How, then, can the Christian school or college express its basic convictions? Having taken for its integrating factor the Word of God with its life-giving revelation of Jesus Christ, in what way is Christian education to go about 'doing' this truth? To the answering of these questions we devote ourselves, as we go on to consider how all subjects of study can be related to the Christian frame of reference.

There are two possible approaches to this problem. The first is through the teacher; the second is by way of the particular subject. If the latter method becomes a point-by-point reconciling of the so-called 'secular' fields of knowledge with the Bible and Christian truth, it may be misleading; when it seeks to discover common ground between the two, it is valuable, though lacking the directness of the first method. But to approach the problem of integration initially by way of the teacher is to go to the root of the matter. We take as our starting point, therefore, the teacher instead of the subject.

About a year ago it was my privilege to spend a forenoon with Professor Karl Barth in his study at Basel in Switzerland. During the course of our conversation, we discussed the question now before us. It was Dr. Barth's emphatic opinion that the most effective way to integrate every subject of study with Christianity is through teachers with a genuinely Christian world view, or *Weltbild*, to use his German word. A few weeks later, I had a similar talk with Mr. C. S. Lewis in his rooms at Magdalen College, Oxford. He expressed the same view. The opinions of these distinguished men confirm a conviction that thoughtful Christian educators have held for years. Yes, the crux of the problem lies with the teacher. The fact is inescapable; the world view of the teacher, in so far as he is effective, gradually conditions the world view of the pupil. No man teaches out of a philosophical vacuum. In one way or another, every teacher expresses the convictions he lives by, whether they be spiritually positive or negative.

This is why the school or college that would develop a Christ-centered and Biblically grounded program must fly from its masthead this standard, 'No Christian education * without Christian teachers,' and must never, under any condition, pull its colors down. Compromise of this issue, if persisted in, always results in the progressive de-Christianizing of an institution. Yet such compromise is exactly what is being advocated today.

Listen to the Professor of Christian Ethics at the Pacific School of Religion; writing in *The Christian Century* on the subject, 'Making the Church College Christian,' Dr. Robert E. Fitch says: 'The showdown . . . is when you are confronted by a choice between the tolerant humanist who is a good scholar and a good teacher, and

---

* The word is here used in the institutional sense and applies to education in the avowedly Christian school or college, such as is under consideration in this book.

the true believer who is a somewhat inferior scholar and teacher. If you choose the latter, you discredit both scholarship and God in the eyes of the students . . . If you choose the former, you give evidence at least that a Christian college respects scholarship and teaching. Furthermore, the men on the faculty who are sincere Christians as well as able scholars and teachers are of sufficient calibre to counteract the lack in the humanist. If the president or the dean knows his business and is unafraid of his principles, he chooses the humanist.' [5]

Plausible as this sounds, it is nothing short of surrender to expediency. In the first place, this course of action sets up a false alternative, for it side-steps the fact that it is possible for God to lead administrators to build faculties that are both Christian and competent. In the second place, this course of action is blind to the fact that the humanist cannot possibly teach compatibly with Christianity but is bound to reflect his Godless world view. The practice of such a policy will in the long run pack a faculty with 'tolerant humanists' for the reason that administrators who adopt it will inevitably take the easy way of appointing benevolent unbelievers rather than searching persistently and prayerfully for teachers who are both scholars and Christians. And who would be so bold as to deny that there are

such and to say that in a country the size of
the United States they cannot be found?

3. But Christians Are Not Immune to
Secularism

If the Christian teacher is so important, we
must think for a few moments about the kind of
world view most faculty members in our Christian schools and colleges have. Let us begin with
the climate of opinion in American education today — secular, naturalistic, man-centered, not
God-centered, taking for its dynamic an almost
religious idealization of democracy. Go through
the faculties of even the evangelical institutions,
and the majority will be found to have been
trained during their most formative years in
schools the educational philosophy of which is
of the earth. Likewise, a fair percentage will have
had their higher education in the teachers' colleges or secular liberal arts colleges and uni-
versities. This is not to say that everyone who
goes to a secular college comes out with a secular
world view. It is possible for deeply committed
Christians to maintain their Christian world
view in an indifferent or hostile atmosphere. But
to do so they must be consciously alert to the
secular pressures about them and they must be
living disciplined Christian lives. Realism com-
pels the admission that all too few Christian stu-

dents in secular colleges are so alerted and disciplined and that all too few of them, therefore, escape heavy inroads of secularism in their thinking.*

On the other hand, a good number of teachers in Christian institutions have themselves gone to Christian colleges. Even in Christian colleges, however, there has been all too little correlation between Christianity and so-called secular subjects. Add to this the fact that the vast majority of textbooks are written from a point of view that fails to relate all truth to God, and we can see that to some degree even our Christian teachers reflect the secularism of our age.

How could the situation be otherwise? The intellectual atmosphere in which their minds have developed has in good part been worldly. Though they themselves have received newness of life through faith in Christ, the categories of thought in which they have for years been nurtured are not so readily sloughed off. The fact is that this mundane, humanistic philosophy is more pervasive than most of us have begun to realize. A while ago I was asked to address a Christian teachers' institute near Philadelphia. In her letter of invitation, the chairman made this discerning statement: 'Most of us evangelicals,

* For further discussion of this problem see the Appendix.

though well grounded in fundamental doctrines, had received educations in general subjects in which God was omitted and thus denied; so that as we under God educate the children, we must be allowing Him to re-educate us.'

It is encouraging that there are some who have awakened to this need for the re-education of even Christian teachers. Among them is the Reverend Mark Fakkema of the National Association of Christian Schools. Mr. Fakkema's syllabus[6] of a basic Christian philosophy of education is consistent and clear. His lectures, delivered in a number of colleges and seminaries throughout the country, have opened the eyes of many teachers who, though regenerate individuals themselves, have never realized that they have been teaching in part at least out of the prevalent humanistic frame of reference.

The Reverend E. A. de Bordenave gives a similar view arrived at by certain Episcopal educators. In a paper published by the National Preparatory School Committee,[7] he writes in reference to a group of Protestant Episcopal church schools: 'This secular religion [the reigning philosophy of modern education] was the point of view from which all textbooks are written, except some of those used in sacred studies. It was the point of view from which nearly all of our faculties had been educated. It was the point of view of most of our parents, Board of Trustees, and to an amazing extent, even of those of us who . . . espouse the Christian faith! This secular faith — which is the real faith of America — infests and corrupts all of us and all of our schools. It permeates the very air we breathe!'

The picture is not overdrawn, nor does it apply only to Episcopal schools.* If the facts were known, it would be seen to apply also to some schools and colleges that, with a strong emphasis upon Bible courses, chapel services, and revivalism, have the name of being outstandingly Christian, though in reality there is too little difference between their teaching of most subjects and that of the teaching in a secular school or state university, except for the fact that in the Christian school classes may be opened by prayer.

What can be done about the situation? The answer is that a great deal can be done about it, providing our Christian education will pay the twofold price of hard thinking plus hard work. One thing is certain; no superficial remedies will suffice. We must go to the root of the problem. And that means nothing short of a reconstruction of attitudes that have through the years become habitual. Instead of spending time in discussing

* A similar point of view has been expressed by other groups, notably the Christian Reformed Church and also the Missouri Synod Lutherans.

side issues, Christian faculties need to investigate the extent to which the secular climate of opinion has drifted into their own minds and colored their own teaching. Such an investigation will be disquieting. It may even result in revisions of cherished presentation of subject matter. But it must be done. In Christian philosophy it is either all or nothing; there are no halfway measures, despite the often unconscious attempt, on the part of many of us, to compromise. We must, in short, see once and for all that St. Paul's challenging phrase, 'bringing into captivity every thought to the obedience of Christ,' [8] is no empty rhetoric; it applies to the whole of Christian education, and is a realizable ideal.

4. *Integration through the Teacher*

Let us look hard at the Christian teacher. When he became a Christian through regeneration, he did not instantaneously receive a completely developed world view; rather was it implanted in germ or in embryo. Just as there are believers who exhibit little growth (the New Testament calls them 'babes' [9]), so there are others who, when it comes to the development of a consistent frame of reference, remain comparative infants. On the other hand, there are some who do grow. After his conversion, St. Paul spent years of solitude in Arabia, and following that sojourn became by inspiration the great systematizer of apostolic Christianity. Augustine developed a close-knit view of Christian truth, as did Calvin, Edwards, and, more recently, Hodge, and Strong, while in our own day men like Barth in Europe, and in this country Chafer and Berkhof for the conservatives and Tillich and Niebuhr for the liberals, have systematized truth as they have seen it.

To expect achievement of this kind from all Christian teachers is obviously impossible. But it is not only possible but also quite reasonable to expect of Christian teachers a world view intelligently understood and held with conviction. For the evangelical teacher that world view rests, as we have seen, first of all upon God's written revelation, though it draws also upon his revelation in nature. It can be built up through that personal study of the Word of God to which every believer is obligated; through the study of great Christian thinkers; and, as has already been suggested, through faculty discussion of the Christian frame of reference.

Of the foregoing, by far the most important is the personal study of the Word of God. It is a sad fact that the Protestant principle of the competence of the individual believer to interpret the Bible under the guidance of the Spirit is so frequently honored only in the breach. Many

Christians of today are notoriously lazy-minded. Too often the Protestant layman relies solely upon his minister for the understanding and, if the truth be told, even for the reading of his Bible. Such secondhand acquaintance with God's Word can never form a man's thinking upon revelational lines. Even among evangelicals who read the Bible and attend Bible conferences as well as church, there is an excess of reliance upon what other men say about the Word of God instead of upon what it says directly to the individual. In all honesty, it must be admitted that no teacher or minister who does not have the Bible at the center of his life and thought to the extent of living daily in this book can hope to develop a Christian frame of reference.

Some years ago Professor Charles Grosvenor Osgood of Princeton wrote a little book called *Poetry As a Means of Grace* in which he recommended an intimate acquaintance with any one of the great poets as an antidote to modern materialism. 'Choose this author,' he said, 'as friends are chosen . . . think of him daily in odd moments. Read a bit of him as often as you can, until at least parts of him become part of yourself. Do not consult other books or people by way of explaining him any more than you can help. Know him first of all. Let him explain himself. What you thus come to know in him will every day seem new and fresh; every recourse to him brings forth new thought, new feeling, new application, new aspects of things familiar. He becomes an antiseptic agent against all the agencies that tend to make life sour, stale, and insipid.' [10] In this plea for living fellowship with some great poet, Professor Osgood has also expressed the way in which we Christians should use our Bible. We might add, if for a student of literature poetry can exercise this remedial effect, how much more will the Bible do for the Christian who learns to live in its pages.

At this point, I speak from personal experience. For many years I have worked in daily fellowship with a skilled teacher of English. His knowledge of literature is of a breadth and depth possessed by few university professors. His classes provide an experience upon which every graduate of the school where he teaches looks back with appreciation. There is no question of this man's professional competence; when he teaches Shakespeare or Milton, he does so with authority born of long and loving familiarity with their works. And all the time there is another book in which, because he is a devoted Christian, he lives in a sense different from his devotion to the English classics. Not only is his heart in the Bible; through his daily use and constant study of it, the Bible has literally formed his mind. Such a man

does not make brief journeys from English literature to the Bible. Despite his constant handling
of literature, his true intellectual and spiritual
home is in the Word of God. Nor is he any less
competent in English because of this fact. Rather
is his teaching of a so-called secular subject en-
riched, because he comes to it with a genuinely
Christian world view. Such a man indulges in
no forced 'reconciliations' between English and
Christianity; instead there is in his teaching a
natural communication of Christian allusions
and attitudes, flowing from a mind and person-
ality steeped in the Bible.

Look again at this example, drawn, as it is, from
life. It affords a clue to the effective integration of
Christianity with the entire curriculum. Join me,
if you will, in following that clue in the field of
education with which I am most familiar — the
independent secondary school. Such schools,
while largely outnumbered by the public high
schools, are significant out of all proportion to
their size. They have the precious freedom to
work in fields not usually cultivated by the public
school, and in respect to Christian teaching they
can go all the way. Their contribution to our
country, already great, is still small compared
with what it might be, were more of them openly
and unashamedly to use their freedom to develop
really Christian programs.

It is a characteristic of these schools to give religion a place in the curriculum. The difficulty is that their classes in religion are in most cases isolated from the other studies. Like small islands of spiritual truth, they stand in the midst of a secular curriculum. Instead of being organically united with the classes in mathematics, literature, science, or history, they are effectively insulated from them. They stand as strongholds for religion in our modern education; but they are too much like the moated castles dotting the British countryside, beautiful and venerable, adding an aura of by-gone splendor to the scene, yet cut off from everyday life.*

The problem is to fill in the moat and bring Christianity out of its venerable castle. To this end, I suggest a plan designed to make Christianity and the Bible the living center of the curriculum. Bold as it may seem, it is not theoretical; it has been tried in the actual experience of school life and has proved effective.

5. *Bible Teachers in 'Secular' Departments*

Briefly the plan is this. The Christian school that believes all truth to be God's truth and that is serious about making Christ and the Bible in-

* The same thing applies to most evangelical schools and colleges; in them the Bible department likewise tends to isolation.

tegral to its curriculum must give up the concept of a completely separate Bible department. Instead it must seek and develop devoted Christian teachers who, along with competency in mathematics, science, languages, or social studies, are able also to give instruction in Bible. Such teachers, particularly on the secondary level, need not necessarily be technically trained as Biblical scholars, although such training is valuable. They must, however, like the Christian English teacher mentioned above, be individuals whose primary spiritual and intellectual residence is in the Bible. On every Christian faculty, there will be certain teachers able and willing to take a class in Bible conjointly with their other work. A single such teacher in each of the major departments is a goal at which to aim. In point of fact, even a partial attainment of that goal will go far toward making Christian truth the vital center of the curriculum.

There is a reason for this. The teacher of history, mathematics, or science who also teaches Bible is concerned with the presentation of God's truth as set forth in the ultimate seat of spiritual authority. Through his class in Bible, he is not only in constant contact with the Book, as every living Christian ought to be; he is actually working with Bible truth, clarifying it in his own mind, seeking to communicate its meaning faithfully and effectively to his pupils. Out of that experience there is bound to come an awareness of the relation of the Word of God to his other subjects. Correlation of Christianity with his regular teaching will be natural and intuitive, not forced and calculated. The more such a plan is extended, the more thorough will be the integration throughout the whole course of study. Like a magnet the Bible will act as a spiritual polarizing agent for the other studies.*

There are objections to this plan. Some may say, for instance, that the Bible is too difficult a subject to be taught by any but experts. A knowledge of the whole field of Biblical literature and exegesis, acquaintance with the original languages, understanding of the intricacies of historical criticism, systematic training in theology and in the philosophy of religion — all these are necessary, it is claimed, for effective Bible teaching. Now without denying the value of such training, which really amounts to the equivalent

* The principle operates whenever a teacher of secular subjects seriously studies his Bible for any purpose whatever. For example, there may be in a Christian school teachers of socalled secular subjects who are effective lay-preachers. Such preaching demands Bible study and this study will inevitably affect, perhaps unconsciously but none the less vitally, the teacher's presentation of his regular subject. This is why the teacher in a Christian school who is an active church or Sunday School worker is so valuable.

of a seminary course, we must declare the objection to be invalid. There will always be a place for the specialist in Bible study; certainly the school that develops its Bible teachers from among its regular faculty needs at least one technically trained man as a guide and center of reference. For the teacher, however, who along with his other classes takes a course or two in Bible it is another matter, providing he is practiced in the art as well as the theory of teaching and provided he is in earnest regarding his Bible. The experienced teacher who can control and interest a class in science can, out of prayerful and faithful study, interest a class in the Word of God. It is being done by some teachers every Lord's Day in some Sunday Schools. It can also be done on weekdays by professional teachers who are devoted to the Bible and deeply concerned with acquainting their students with its message.

Another objection is raised on purely practical grounds. The plan of tying Scripture into the whole course of study through developing Bible teachers within the various departments sounds good, we are told, but in actuality it is impossibly utopian. The hard facts of teacher procurement will prevent anything like its effective realization. In answer to this objection, may I remind you in all humility that this plan of the develop-

ment of Bible teachers within the school is not
proposed by an armchair theorist. Most of what
I know of education has been gained in the everyday experience of administering a Christian
school for thirty years. It is perfectly true that genuinely Christian teachers are hard to get — how
hard none but an administrator who for a long
time has coped with this problem knows. Just as
Rome was not built in a day, so a vitally Christian
faculty is not assembled overnight. It grows
through a period of years. All of us engaged in the
administration of schools and colleges committed
to definite doctrinal standards have been disap-
pointed in teachers who have given us the right
answers but whose day-by-day walk has mani-
fested the wrong life. In building a faculty there
is no substitute for experience, and, in view of our
human fallibility, a certain amount of trial and
error is unavoidable. Nevertheless, it is surely
within the bounds of possibility to assemble a faculty made up wholly of professionally competent
teachers who are vitally Christian, using the ad-
jective in the sense of personal knowledge of
Christ as Lord and Saviour. Unanimity of de-
nomination is not essential; unanimity of faith is.
Once a faculty of this kind has been built, or,
shall we say, once it is clearly in the process of
being built, there is every possibility of recruit-

ing from within its ranks those who can be developed into effective Bible teachers.

The key to such development is a compelling vision of the greatness of the task and a realization of the obligation to do it. Admittedly, such work is not for everyone; it is not for every faculty member in even the best Christian school. But surely in any faculty composed of teachers for whom Bible reading is no mere pious duty but spiritual food and drink without which the soul cannot grow, there will be found some who will undertake it.

The challenge is a great one; it is for the Christian teacher who in all he does seeks first the glory of God. Yes, the task is hard. And in its very difficulty lies its appeal. As Professor Whitehead once said, 'The art of education is never easy. To surmount its difficulties . . . is a task worthy of the highest genius. It is the training of souls.' [11] Few in Christian education — and we must include the ministry with its teaching function — would claim genius on any level, let alone the highest. We have something better. We have the certainty that the Lord whom we serve and whose we are will never fail, as we look to the guidance of the Spirit, to give us the measure of wisdom and strength needed for the doing of His will.

Notes

1. *The Adventures of Don Quixote,* by Miguel de Cervantes Saavedra, translated by J. M. Cohen, Middlesex, 1950, p. 490.
2. Romans 1:18–23.
3. This description of the carbon clock is based upon 'Detectives of Time,' N. J. Berrill, *The Atlantic Monthly,* July 1953. The material here presented was kindly checked for accuracy by Prof. J. Laurence Kulp of Columbia University.
4. Titus 2:13.
5. *The Christian Century,* 10 September 1952. Used by permission.
6. Published by the National Association of Christian Schools, 542 South Dearborn Street, Chicago 5, 1953.
7. Published by the National Preparatory School Committee, 347 Madison Avenue, New York 17, April 1949.
8. II Corinthians 10:5.
9. I Corinthians 3:1; Hebrews 5:13.
10. *Poetry As a Means of Grace,* Charles Grosvenor Osgood, Princeton, 1941, p. 22. Used by permission.
11. *The Aims of Education and Other Essays,* by Alfred North Whitehead, New York, reprint 1949, p. 62.

CHAPTER THREE

THE SUBJECT AND THE TRUTH

'Finally, brethren, whatsoever things
are true . . . think on these things.'
Philippians 4:8

1. *From Teacher to Subject*

ONCE a school embraces the policy of giving
classes in Bible to Christian teachers of other
subjects, it is on the way to integrating Christianity with its entire curriculum. In such a school
Biblical truth will soon cross departmental bar-
riers and, to use a biological figure, pollinate the
so-called 'secular' studies. How far this cross-
pollination goes will depend on the extent to
which teachers are rooted and grounded in the
Word of God.

'Rooted and grounded' — to most minds the
phrase suggests the *status quo,* whereas the Christian who is actually 'rooted and grounded' is
growing in the truth. If his roots strike deep into
Scripture, they do so for nourishment. Such a
basis for living means much more than doctrinal
correctness; it implies increasing knowledge of
divine truth, a desire to communicate it to others,
and practicing it in daily life.

The foregoing, while stressing the teacher, also serves another purpose — that of being a hinge upon which discussion may turn, as we move from teacher to subject in order to investigate the relation between Christianity and other fields of learning. The transition requires careful thinking. Because, for example, some have insisted upon a forced, point-by-point reconciling of the Bible and science, it by no means follows that the two have nothing in common. Nor does the fact that the chief thrust in integration comes through the teacher make the broad connections between revealed and natural truth any the less important. Quite the opposite — they are indispensable guides to the unity of all learning under God.

Passing, then, from teacher to subject, we face the necessity of selecting from the many fields of knowledge a few for discussion. Instead of taking the major areas one by one and passing them in review — a procedure out of the question because of limitations of space — we shall begin with the subject hardest to integrate with Christianity. After this, a second subject will be considered as representative of areas in which integration is more easily achieved. And finally we shall go on to a third subject which will open up another but related field, that of aesthetics.

2. *The Hardest Subject To Integrate*

What is the hardest subject to integrate with Christianity? Most students of Christian education emphasize history, literature, and science, fields in which integration is most readily achieved. But almost to a man they shy away from mathematics. So the question is asked, usually in expectation of a negative reply: 'Can anyone really discover common ground between mathematics and Christianity?'

The answer is affirmative. To cite distinguished authority, Pascal, one of the greatest mathematical minds the world has known,[1] discovered such ground. In 1658 or 1659 he wrote his discourse, entitled *The Mind of the Geometrician.*[2] A study of this discourse shows that the basis common to the Christian frame of reference and mathematics — in this instance, geometry — lies on the epistemological level. Pascal saw clearly that geometry, despite its precise definition of 'self-evident' truths, can never of itself verify these truths for the simple reason that it is based upon things that are at bottom unverifiable. He recognized the application of this principle to such fundamental concepts as time, space, motion, number, and equality. Furthermore, he anticipated the modern scientific view, as set forth by Max Planck, that even causality cannot be proved, though according to Planck it remains 'the most valuable pointer we possess in order to find a path through the confusion of events.' [3] For Pascal the task of the geometer was 'the art of demonstrating those truths that have already been discovered and of clarifying them in such a manner that their truth is inconvertible.' [4] As he says, 'All these truths [including 'the two infinities which are to be found in all things, infinite largeness and infinite smallness'] cannot be proved. However, since the quality which makes them incapable of proof is not their obscurity, but rather their extreme obviousness, that lack of proof is not a defect but rather a mark of excellence. From this we see that geometry cannot define objects nor prove principles, but the one and very weighty reason is that both possess an extreme inherent clarity which convinces reason more strongly than does argumentation.' [5]

The question now arises, 'How, then, are these truths of mathematics discovered?' According to Pascal they are found out through intuition. We know them through the heart; they are instinctive. As he put it in a famous aphorism, 'The heart, and not reason, senses God.' [6] The same thing holds for divine truths. As Pascal went on to say in *The Art of Persuasion*, they too 'have their places infinitely above nature. God alone can place them in the soul and do this in a manner pleasing to Himself.' [7] Pascal's approach to geometry is therefore like the approach of the theologian to divinity. In his system, 'Any proof of the existence of God presupposes faith in God.' [8]

Now such a view raises an impressive objection against the cocksure rationalism of the materialist and naturalist. Those 'self-evident' axioms that are the raw material of the geometer's thought — and the principle holds for our modern forms of non-Euclidian geometry and for other branches of mathematics as well — are essentially unprovable. One accepts them as valid and true, and they can then be defined and used, even though they remain unverifiable. The whole vast structure of mathematics, with its myriad applications throughout manifold areas of science and of life, can be built upon them.

It is the same with Christianity. Its basic postulates are likewise unprovable in human logic, though not in the experience of the heart. Once we submit to them through faith, they too can be defined and used, so as to bear fruit in the illimitable field of Christian life and character. They also 'possess an extreme inherent clarity which convinces reason more strongly than does argumentation.' [9]

There are, of course, between mathematics and the Christian view, areas of agreement other than this epistemological one. There is for example, the existence of number * and order not only in the world but also throughout the universe.

Commenting on Galileo's statement, 'Nature's great book is written in mathematical language,' Sir James Jeans said, 'So true is it that no one except a mathematician can hope fully to understand those branches of science which try to unravel the fundamental nature of the universe.' [12] And when he remarked that 'from the intrinsic evidence of his creation the Great Architect of the universe now begins to appear as a great mathematician,' [13] Jeans was only expressing for the modern mind what ancient philosophy had stated in the two words, 'God geometrizes.' The whole science of astronomy is based upon the mathematical accuracy of planetary and stellar movements. Crystallography is solid geometry in the mineral and chemical realm demonstrated

---

* That there is a spiritual symbolism in the basic numbers is a Biblical fact perhaps better known to the mediaeval than to the modern mind. In his great work, *Religious Art in the Thirteenth Century*, Emile Mâle has a remarkable treatment of the symbolism of numbers [10] in relation to the cathedrals which he aptly calls 'the Bible of stone.' And Dante, to turn to the greatest poet of the Middle Ages, finds in numbers a wealth of spiritual meaning. His *Divine Comedy* is a trilogy, each section of which, consisting of thirty-three cantos, is marked by symbolic numbers (the nine circles of the Inferno, the seven terraces of Purgatory, and the nine heavens of Paradise).[11]

with a beauty and perfection beyond description. Each note of the musical scale has its exact number of vibrations a minute. The discovery by Pythagoras in the sixth century B.C. that the musical intervals depend on 'certain arithmetical ratios of lengths of strings at the same tension . . . powerfully contributed to the idea that "all things are numbers" ' [14] — that number is, as Pythagoras taught, at the core of the universe. So the musical scale undergirds, as it were, the thought of the man who first made mathematics the foundation of all the sciences. Moreover, the very elements themselves follow a mathematical order. And when Job referred to 'the treasures of the snow,' [15] the microscope was undreamed of, yet what riches of geometrical intricacy it reveals in one square inch of glittering flakes!

In the light of such wonders, we have no business to think of mathematics as an entirely secular branch of learning. The old-fashioned designation of 'pure mathematics' or 'pure science' is no longer valid. As Dean Gauss of Princeton pointed out,[16] such terminology rested upon the assumption that these 'pure' subjects 'belonged in a self-sufficient world of their own.' But this is not true; the world of mathematical precision is God's world, and it is His in a unique identity.

Writing of his student days, Professor S. R. Williams of Amherst College gives us this moving reminiscence: 'Never would that boy forget the excitement and thrill he experienced when, as a college student, he sat for the first time at the eyepiece of a transit instrument in order to find the time of night from the stars. Years before, the astronomers had figured . . . that so many hours, minutes, seconds, and fractions of a second past midnight, the star Alpha Cassiopeiae would move through the line of sight of the transit instruments when the telescope was elevated so many degrees, minutes, and seconds of arch above the horizon. In an adjoining room a sidereal clock was beating out star seconds. Close by the observer these beats were being recorded on a revolving drum called a chronograph. By means of an electric key the observer could superimpose upon the record of the clock beats the exact moment that Alpha Cassiopeiae passed the meridian line in the field of view.

'As the boy peers into the telescope it yet lacks some seconds of the calculated time, but breathlessly, with trembling hand on the electric key, he keeps his eye glued to the eyepiece. Perhaps the star has lost time somewhere or else sprinted along on its journey, and won't arrive on schedule. Best to keep on the alert! The first glimpse of the field shows no star, but as the seconds drag along, suddenly — yes, there she is just coming into sight at one side of the field of view, exactly

according to the timetable! Steady now, get set
— click — Alpha Cassiopeiae has just gone under the central wire . . . The clock, man-made,
may gain or lose, but never Alpha Cassiopeiae.
The heavens had declared the glory of God, and
the firmament had revealed his handiwork. Law
and order had once more been demonstrated as
the guiding principle of the universe.

'After studying the theory of probability, the
callow youth . . . decided that no system could
run on a chance basis and perform like Alpha
Cassiopeiae . . . the movements of celestial
bodies were all on such a vast, complex scale that
only a superintellect, he felt, could keep in order
such a system of regularity and precision. The
universe revealed itself as a purposive one in its
behavior.' [17]

Surely the conclusion is inevitable that a subject so close to the way in which God works and
— we say it reverently — so close to the way in
which He thinks is well inside the pattern of His
truth. Consequently, it follows that the Christian
teacher of mathematics must know such things as
the common ground of unprovable knowledge
shared by mathematics and Christianity, the pres-
ence of number and order throughout nature and
art, and the perfect congruity of the stars with
mathematical calculation. Out of these facts and
others like them, he can show his pupils more

than is generally realized. Young people can wonder at the wisdom of the God of mathematical truth quite as much as they marvel at the Creator of the great mountains, the restless oceans, and the star-decked heavens.

3. *The Christian Integration of Literature*

What we have just pointed out respecting the common ground of mathematics and the Biblical view makes no pretense to completeness; it is offered simply as a road into territory needing to be explored by Christian thought. Nor will our second avenue of investigation, which turns our attention from mathematics to literature, be treated with any greater completeness.

Here is a field in which the possibilities of integration are as numerous as they are obvious. There are so many ways in which literature, whether in English or in any other language, may be correlated with Christianity that the problem is one of selection. This is true because books, particularly of a creative kind, are in good measure a mirror held up to life, being almost as varied as life itself. As for Christianity, it gives men nothing less than life more abundant. The common ground between Christianity and literature is therefore as comprehensive as life itself. Both are concerned with the springs of human character; both have to do with the outward manifestation of that character in human action. The analogy, however, must not be pressed too far. The integration of the Bible and literature is not that of seemingly diverse fields, as with mathematics and Scripture; it is an integration of two sections of the same field, for the Bible is itself literature. Nevertheless, the integration is not that of equals, because it must never be forgotten that Scripture is more than a human book. Human it certainly is, but by reason of the factor of inspiration it is something else as well. The difference between it and the writings of men is like the difference between the Person of Christ and the person of man. Christ is fully man; in fact, He is the only whole, or complete, man unmarred by any imperfection. As such, He is the ideal for us imperfect human beings and at the same time stands in judgment upon our lack of wholeness. But along with His perfect human nature, Christ is fully divine. He is Deity manifest in the flesh, very God of very God, and in this category He differs from us not only in degree but above all in kind.

Look now at the Bible in comparison with human literature. The former is human, but it is human with a wholeness and soundness of outlook no other book has. At the same time it is also divine. Through the ages Christians have recognized its unique inspiration; the life experience of countless believers bears witness to the fact that the Bible is of a different order from any other book. In and through its words, the Spirit of God works as in no other literature. The Christian teacher has in the Bible not only a model but also a frame of reference for all other books. When it comes to the heart of things, this book is the norm. In literary form it takes highest rank, though it is an ancient and Oriental book. But beautiful as its language is, men speak and write differently today.

And so, while we admire and appreciate the Bible as literature, its most important function is on another and higher level. Here, in the plainest meaning of the words, is the book of life. Here is the book of morality, the volume that uncovers the springs of human action, whether good or evil. Here is the book the truth of which judges us. Here is the literature of power in a far loftier sense than Matthew Arnold realized. For this book contains the only dynamic that can change a bad man into a good man, a sinner into a saint. It is the book of Christ. Through its pages the living Saviour is mediated to our hearts by the Spirit in a manner wholly unique. It is, in fine, the book that measures everything, the yardstick of all literature, the touchstone of the ages.

The problem of the integration of literature with the Christian world view can therefore be solved only by teachers who are established in the Word of God. In sober fact, such teachers are solving it in many a classroom today. There is no lack, as has already been shown, of points of contact between literature and Christianity; as the Lord Jesus said in another connection, 'the field is the world.' [18]

This world in which we live is full of those moral and spiritual choices, the interplay of which is the stuff out of which great writing is made. In the words of Professor Knight of Yale, 'No teacher need force literature into concern with a moral pattern; literature will force that concern on him. Without the tension of alternate choice there can be no literature.' [19] To say that the Bible is the book wherein 'the tension of alternate choice' is most fully and perfectly set forth is not debatable. From the major tension between God and Satan, good and evil, salvation and condemnation, to the minor tensions within the lives of God's children as well as within the lives of unbelievers, Scripture is concerned with moral choices. Stevenson gives us Dr. Jekyll and Mr. Hyde, but St. Paul in a single mighty paragraph at the end of the seventh chapter of the Epistle to the Romans* lays bare once and for all

* 'For that which I do I allow not: for what I would, that do I not; but what I hate, that do I. If then I do that which I would not, I consent unto the law that it is good. Now then

the conflict of the two natures within man and anticipates some of the deepest insights of modern psychology.

It follows, therefore, that in the understanding of literature the non-Christian interpreter is under a crucial handicap. This handicap is the lack of a Biblical view of sin. Academic and literary circles today include a number of teachers and writers who would say with President Harold Taylor of Sarah Lawrence College, 'philosophy which is adequate for life . . . will deny the superstition that man is sinful.' [21] Or even if the hard facts of this troubled world compel a certain reluctant recognition of sin, these interpreters have little understanding of its real nature as an offense against a God, who is holy, just, and loving. For them whole areas throughout great litera-

it is no more I that do it, but sin that dwelleth in me. For I know that in me (that is, in my flesh,) dwelleth no good thing: for to will is present with me; but how to perform that which is good I find not. For the good that I would I do not; but the evil which I would not, that I do. Now if I do that I would not, it is no more I that do it, but sin that dwelleth in me. I find then a law, that, when I would do good, evil is present with me. For I delight in the law of God after the inward man: But I see another law in my members, warring against the law of my mind, and bringing me into captivity to the law of sin which is in my members. O wretched man that I am! who shall deliver me from the body of this death? I thank God through Jesus Christ our Lord. So then with the mind I myself serve the law of God; but with the flesh the law of sin.' [20]

ture cannot even be fully understood in their own right. An example is George Santayana's essay on 'Religion in Shakespeare.' In it, as Professor Roland M. Frye of Emory University has shown,[22] the distinguished philosopher, ignoring the Christian view of evil which was so well known to Shakespeare, cannot help but miss some of the very deepest levels of this great writer's meaning.

But for every teacher of literature whose mind and heart are rooted and grounded in the Word of God, the secret of integrating Christianity and literature is an open one. Such a teacher, provided he is able to communicate knowledge and to lead his students to discover it for themselves, can hardly escape a high degree of integration. It will surely come, as he sees the books under consideration, whether Shakespeare or Hemingway, Goethe or Tolstoy, in the penetrating light of the Bible.

4. *The Fine Arts — Music*

From literature to the fine arts — the transition is a natural one. Literature itself impinges upon the fine arts through poetry and drama. And the fine arts are an essential element of education; without some knowledge of them, no education, least of all a Christian one, is complete. This being the case, the problem of integration relates to the arts just as to mathematics, science, history, or any other subject. Again limitations of space compel a selection. In this instance the choice is plain. If one from among the arts must be singled out for special study, it is music. There are good reasons for this. In the first place, music is par excellence the Christian art. From Genesis to Revelation, it runs throughout Scripture. Not only that, music will have a leading place in eternity, according to the inspired visions of John on Patmos.[23] Moreover, when we come to the matter of worship here and now, music is a vital factor in preparing the heart for God's truth.

Important as these offices of music are, they are not the only way it speaks to the spirit of man. Many of the greatest compositions, even though outwardly secular, are of a spiritual nature. The slow movement of many a Beethoven sonata, quartet, or symphony moves on a lofty religious plane. In the works of other great composers such as Bach, Mozart, Haydn, Mendelssohn, and Brahms, there are similar passages. It is significant that hymnology has drawn upon the classic composers for some of its finest tunes.[24] No, there is nothing obscure about the relation of music to Christianity. The common ground between the two requires occupation, not discovery. But the moment we begin to occupy that ground and do something about the place of music in Christian life and work, we run into difficulty.

One summer day, several leaders of the 1952 Conference conducted by the International Fellowship of Evangelical Students at Jugenheim near Darmstadt, Germany, were discussing music. In the course of the conversation, I said that for me there is in the music used in evangelical work much that is trite, sentimental, and even vulgar. But, I went on, I had come to the conclusion that to condemn it would be wrong, because it is apparently a source of blessing to many, who, innocent of any real musical appreciation, are helped by it. In short, I had determined not to be a musical snob, even though to a cultivated taste much that was played and sung in conjunction with the presentation of the Gospel was aesthetically disagreeable. Immediately there came a challenge from a distinguished leader of British evangelicalism. 'My dear fellow,' he exclaimed, 'you mustn't say that! Don't you see you are saying that the end justifies the means, and that is positively wrong?'

Was my British friend right? Is the use of third-rate tunes and worse harmony in our churches, youth meetings, evangelistic campaigns, and education, simply on the ground of results, really so wrong? Is this kind of music unworthy to be associated with the Gospel? And should it, therefore, be politely bowed out of our educational institutions where Christian leadership is being trained? These are important questions. An answer requires a brief excursion into a field almost untouched by present-day Christian thought — that of aesthetics.

The tie between music and religion is an ancient one, going back to the beginning of civilization when, according to Genesis, Jubal invented the harp and organ, an achievement classed by Calvin among the 'excellent gifts of the Holy Spirit.' * Nor is music, despite the great development of the art during the last three hundred years, a new thing in our Christian era. As the distinguished composer, Paul Hindemith, pointed out in his Charles Eliot Norton Lectures at Harvard, Augustine wrestled with the coordination of music with Christianity, as did Boethius also, and both came to conclusions of lasting value.[26]

According to Augustine (*De Musica*. Book vi.) for Christian believers music is more than pleasing sounds. Such sounds are meaningless until we 'include them in our own mental activity and use their fermenting quality to turn our soul towards everything noble, superhuman, and ideal.' [27] In other words, we are obliged to use

* It should not be forgotten that Calvin accorded music an important place under the doctrine of common grace.[25]

music for our soul's betterment, because 'like religious belief, music creates in us most easily a state of willingness towards this betterment.' [28] And Boethius in the initial sentence of his *De Institutione Musica* puts in a nutshell the gist of his view: 'Music is part of our human nature,' he says; 'it has the power either to improve or debase our character.' [29] The two views, that of Augustine and that of Boethius, differ in their estimate of the inherent moral and spiritual influence of music; but in respect to the tie between music and the moral side of man they are at one. Both imply that music cannot be morally neutral.

The principle is not just a curiosity of ancient thought but a key to the spiritual meaning of music. With this in mind, we set it alongside an even older view, that of Aristotle. For him, as for other Greek philosophers, music was the most 'imitative' of the arts. By 'imitative' Aristotle did not mean that the artist or composer copies nature, but that he must 'imitate things as they ought to be.' [30] In Aristotle's view, as Professor Butcher says, 'music in reflecting character, moulds and influences it.' [31]

Right here we discover a link with the Christian use of music today. In Greek thought about music, 'much of its meaning was derived from the association it called up, and from the emotional atmosphere which surrounded it. It was associ-

ated with definite occasions and solemnities . . .
and attached to well-known words.' [32] This is
something very like the place of music among the
Hebrews and early Christians. After all, the Old
Testament over and over again associated music
with worship, as in the Psalms and in the prophets; the New Testament also recognizes it, when
St. Paul writes of 'speaking to yourselves in
psalms and hymns and spiritual songs, singing
and making melody in your heart to the Lord,' [33]
and in another place speaks of 'teaching and ad-
monishing one another in psalms and hymns and
spiritual songs, singing with grace in your
hearts.' [34]

But our thought leaps across the centuries, and
we exclaim: 'How similar to this ancient view of
music is its use, not only in our churches, but also
in evangelism! Think of a Sankey in the Moody
campaigns with his irresistible singing of *The
Ninety and Nine*, or a Beverly Shea in a Billy
Graham meeting, reaching multitudes with *I'd
Rather Have Jesus*.' Such songs, while musically
undistinguished, need no defense. In preparing
the heart for divine truth, they serve as hand-
maids of the Gospel.

Writing on the history of the evangelical student movment at Cambridge University, the
Rev. J. C. Pollock quotes a moving example of
the power of a simple Gospel hymn. The words

are from the pen of the distinguished scholar, A. C. Benson, son of the Archbishop of Canterbury, and describe the singing of Ira Sankey when he and Moody held meetings for the Cambridge students:

'An immense, bilious man with black hair and eyes surrounded by flaccid, pendent baggy wrinkles,' he came forward, 'with an unctuous gesture, and took his place at a small harmonium, placed so near the front of the platform that it looked as if both player and instrument must inevitably topple over; it was inexpressibly ludicrous to behold. Rolling his eyes in an affected manner, he touched a few simple chords, and a marvelous transformation came over the room.

'In a sweet, powerful voice, with an exquisite simplicity combined with irresistible emotion, he sang "There Were Ninety and Nine." The man was transfigured, a deathly hush came over the room, and I felt my eyes fill with tears. His physical repulsiveness slipped from him and left a sincere, impulsive Christian whose simple music spoke straight to the soul.' [35] That is a picture of Gospel music at its best.

After all, there has been a great deal of nonsense written about Gospel music, both pro and con. For example, Dr. A. T. Davison of Harvard in the midst of a slashing attack on Gospel hymns says: 'They still hold a nostalgic place in the affections of a vanishing generation, but in the services of enlightened churches they are never heard.' [36] Well, it is hard to be patient with such an unrealistic appraisal with its supercilious reference to 'a vanishing generation' in contrast to 'enlightened churches.' At the other extreme from this radical disparagement of the Gospel hymn is the statement of a pastor in *The Christian Herald:* 'Bright, happy singing is tonic for the soul.' This is true enough, but what of the next sentence with its deplorably low estimate of the central function of the ministry — 'Preachers will sing more into the kingdom than preach in.' [37] A good singing voice is an asset to any preacher. But the primary fulfillment of the commission to proclaim the Word of God is through the spoken word, not through song.

The truth about Christian music lies midway between the two extremes. The Gospel hymn rightly presented is here to stay; its proper use does not necessarily involve us in justifying the means by the end. On the other hand, there is a great deal of music in favor among evangelicals that justly falls under condemnation; cheap, vulgar, and aesthetically false, its use for good ends does not alter its character. The fact is that American evangelicalism urgently needs to progress to a higher level of music. In the recognition of this need and in doing something about it, Christian education faces a great challenge.

We look, therefore, frankly and sympathetically at the state of music in our churches and educational institutions today. In which direction are we moving? With nation-wide religious broadcasting and television, there has come into Christian work a kind of music and technique of presentation savoring more of Hollywood than of God. Glamour has invaded the proclamation of the Gospel. The deep sincerity of the simple Gospel song has been replaced by a keyboard showiness, a tear-jerking use of the most eloquent of all instruments, the violin, and a sentimental misuse of the innately noble organ, with tremolant pulled out *ad nauseam*. 'Messages' are 'brought' on electric Hawaiian guitars, cowbells, and even musical saws. Great hymns, such as 'When I Survey the Wondrous Cross,' are rattled off in waltz time or adorned with variations of a third-grade musical level. All this is condoned as being catchy and giving the people what they want.

The time has come to climb higher in order to seek a fresh perspective. Must we continue in the rut of aesthetic mediocrity, simply because the third-rate seems to appeal to the crowd? Can anyone seriously imagine some of our attention-getting music as being what St. Paul calls 'spiritual songs'? Has not the time come to tell the truth and admit that these things are nothing but ear-tickling devices, unworthy of association with the grand truths of our redemption?

'But,' some insist, 'this kind of music brings in the people. We've got to have it to get an audience.' Do we? Well, 'The Lutheran Hour,' still heard round the world as in the days of Dr. Walter Maier, is of unquestioned orthodoxy, yet it manages very well without the nervous jingle afflicting some of our Gospel broadcasts. Can it be that we evangelicals are not only aesthetically immature but that we also insist upon remaining so? Have we so far forgotten the apostolic exhortation to 'think on' the things that are 'lovely and of good report' [38] that we by-pass the first-rate in favor of the third-rate? Have we, finally, overlooked the fact that nothing, whether in music or preaching, can possibly be too good for the Lord?

If there is any truth in what has just been said, then Christian education must lead the way to reform. The Bible schools and institutes must rethink their aesthetics in the light of the plain fact that God should have the best. Other Christian schools and colleges have an obligation to strengthen their music departments. They should look to it that all students hear as much great music as possible, and that an increasing number enjoy the creative experience of making good music. And — if the suggestion may be respectfully offered — the theological seminaries might well give music a real place in the curriculum, for among Christian workers the pastor can least of all afford to remain musically illiterate.

At this point, fairness requires the mention of some hopeful signs. Houghton College expresses regret that 'people who dig deep into the truths of the great Christian faith are given to the most superficial music; that Bach, who loved God deeply, receives scant hearing in American fundamental churches.' The college plans a Bach festival once every four years, so that every student generation will hear some of the great works of this most Christian of composers. Westmont College announces a tour of its choir which will sing a program made up of settings from the Psalms, the Song of Solomon, the Gospels, First Corinthians, and Revelation, by Palestrina, Bach, Handel, Mendelssohn, Franck, and modern composers like William Schuman. The St. Olaf College choir has long been famous, and excellent music is sung by the Wheaton and Asbury choirs, to name only a few others. It is to be hoped that these tokens are the beginning of a musical renaissance among evangelicals.

Let there be no misunderstanding. It is not

Gospel hymns that are in question. When it comes to them and their more formal companions, it is not a matter of 'either-or' but of 'both-and.' Each has its place according to the kind of service being conducted. Nor is the answer a willy-nilly imposing of Bach, Beethoven, and Brahms upon the musically untaught, or an insistence upon a dead level of solemnity. There is no place in Christian worship, to say nothing of evangelism, for art for art's sake. In the Church, art must always be in God's service. Surely we have ample scriptural warrant for making 'a joyful noise unto the Lord.' [39] Good music is often happy music, and joy and brightness have their place in worship. The solution is something quite different; it is nothing short of the reversal of a trend that is bringing into worship a kind of music which is neither lovely nor of good report.

The call is for Christian education to lead the way to higher things. But that call will not be fully answered until our schools, colleges, and seminaries espouse a philosophy of music befitting the Gospel. So long as the lower levels of an art so closely linked to man's emotions are cultivated at the expense of the best, we shall continue to have Christian leaders many of whom are deaf to the nobler elements of spiritual song. Evangelicalism is due for a musical reformation. The ref-

ormation will come only when Christian education, having set its face against the cheap in this
greatest of the arts, seeks to develop in its students
response to a level of music worthy of the deep
things of God. Here, as in so much else, we do
well to listen to Martin Luther, who called music
'a noble gift of God next to theology,' and even
went so far as to say: 'We must teach music in
schools; a schoolmaster ought to have skill in
music . . . neither should we ordain young men
as preachers unless they have been well exercised
in music.' 40

Notes

1. This eloquent paragraph from Chateaubriand will remind
   us of the true stature of Pascal: 'Once there was a human
   being who at the age of twelve created mathematics by
   means of bars and circles; who at sixteen wrote the most
   learned treatise on conic sections since the Ancients; who
   at nineteen reduced into a machine, a science which exists
   entirely in the mind; who at twenty-three demonstrated
   the phenomena of atmospheric pressure, and brought to
   nought one of the greatest errors of ancient physics; who,
   at an age when other men have hardly begun to see the
   light, had completed the circle of the human sciences
   and, aware of their nothingness, turned his thoughts to
   religion; who, from that time until his death in his
   thirty-ninth year, always infirm and suffering, molded the
   language which Bossuet and Racine were to speak, and
   gave the model for the most perfect form of wit, as well
   as for the most powerful reasoning; a man finally, who
   during the short intervals in his sufferings solved one of
   the greatest problems of geometry as a pastime, and scrib-

bled on stray bits of paper thoughts which pertain as much to God as to man. This awe-inspiring genius was called Blaise Pascal.' *Genie du christianisme*, by Francois René Chateaubriand, Paris, 1826–31, p. 8.

2. *Great Shorter Works of Pascal*, translated by Emile Cailliet and John C. Blankenagel, Philadelphia, 1948, pp. 189–202. This and the following passages used by permission.
3. Quoted ibid. pp. 29, 30.
4. Ibid. p. 189.
5. Ibid. p. 196.
6. *Pensées*, translated by W. F. Trotter, New York, 1931, p. 78.
7. Op. cit. pp. 202, 203.
8. Ibid. p. 30.
9. Ibid. p. 196.
10. *L'Art religieux du XIIIe siècle en France*, by Emile Mâle, Paris, 1898, pp. 6–18.
11. Ibid. p. 16.
12. *The Mysterious Universe*, by Sir James Jeans, New York, 1930, p. 136.
13. Ibid. p. 144.
14. *Encyclopaedia Britannica*, New York and Chicago, 1938, vol. 18, p. 803.
15. Job 38:22.
16. *The Teaching of Religion in Higher Education*, Christian Gauss, ed., New York, 1951, p. iii.
17. *The Christian Century*, 'The Laws of God: A Physicist's Faith,' 25 February 1953. Used by permission.
18. Matthew 13:38.
19. *College Teaching and Christian Values*, Paul M. Limbert, ed., New York, 1951, p. 141.
20. Romans 7:15–25.
21. *Goals for American Education*, New York, 1950, p. 443.
22. 'Macbeth and the Powers of Darkness,' by Roland M. Frye, *The Emory University Quarterly*, October 1952.
23. Cf. Revelation 5:9; 14:3; 15:3.
24. For example, Palestrina, Bach, Mozart, Beethoven, Weber, Schumann, Mendelssohn.

THE SUBJECT AND THE TRUTH 83

25. *Calvinism*, by Abraham Kuyper, Grand Rapids, 1931, pp. 243, 244.
26. *A Composer's World*, by Paul Hindemith, Cambridge, 1952.
27. Ibid. p. 5.
28. Ibid. p. 5.
29. Ibid. p. 7.
30. *Poetics*, xxv. 1.
31. *Aristotle's Theory of Poetry and Fine Art*, by S. H. Butcher, London, 1920, p. 130.
32. Ibid. p. 130.
33. Ephesians 5:19.
34. Colossians 3:16.
35. *The House of Quiet*, by A. C. Benson, quoted in *A Cambridge Movement*, by J. C. Pollock, London, 1953, p. 64. Used by permission.
36. *Church Music, Illusion and Reality*, by A. T. Davison, Cambridge, 1952, p. 114.
37. *The Christian Herald*, January 1953.
38. Philippians 4:8.
39. Psalm 98:4.
40. *A Compend of Luther's Theology*, Hugh Thomson Kerr, ed., Philadelphia, 1943, p. 147.

CHAPTER FOUR

THE TRUTH BEYOND THE CLASSROOM

'Whatsoever you do in word or deed, do all in the name of the Lord Jesus, giving thanks to God and the Father by him.'
Colossians 3:17

1. *Beyond the Classroom*

ONE of the leading forms of musical composition is the theme and variations, in which the development, varied as it may be, must always be related to the theme. So it is with the structure of these lectures; the theme is the noble one of God's truth, and the continuing aim is to ascertain how various areas of Christian education — the variations, as it were — can be joined to this truth as parts of a living whole.

The figure, though useful, is imperfect. The whole is greater than any of its parts, and education, wide as its scope is, can never be more than part of the truth. Moreover, when we take God's truth for our subject, we have a theme so vast that its fullest exposition can reveal only a fraction of its greatness. For His truth embraces not only this world and everything therein, including all history past, present, and future; it also includes

84

the entire universe from its beginnings in the in-
conceivably distant past to its conclusion in the
unknowable future.

We have, therefore, ample warrant for stepping outside the classroom and looking at some
other problems. Education is more than teachers
and courses. The school has its setting, its environment in which it lives and moves and has its
being; it also has its general policies and practices
beyond the classroom. These are just as much
part of God's truth as the subject matter of the
various courses of study. Thus the process of integration moves from an individual level, as in
the case of the teacher, or from a departmental
level, as in the case of a particular subject, to the
institutional level, in which the school or college
as a whole is involved.

2. *The Extra-curricular Program*

Our first step will take us from the classroom to
those activities which, though commonly called
'extra-curricular,' are yet a vital part of education. The day has long passed, if indeed it was
ever present, when learning meant only what
went on in the classroom and nothing more. The
whole kaleidoscope of activities — clubs and
hobbies, literary and debating societies, publications, dramatics, orchestras, bands, and choirs,
and last, but very far from least, athletics — these

too are part of educational experience. They also have their place within God's truth and, no less than mathematics or science, history or literature, must be united with it.

So numerous are these activities that to deal with them one by one is out of the question. We can, however, discuss principles in relation to a few particular cases. And if, in doing this, we shall seem to be walking on familiar ground and repeating old truths, no apology need be made; there are some things that must be said over and over, and the fact that certain truths are well known does not make them any the less true.

What, then, of the integration of non-athletic activities with a Christian program of education? The problem is first one of selection. What activities are permissible? Which ones are not? Clearly, certain activities in good standing in secular schools have no place in Christian education. And if, through some oversight, they do find their way in, they can never be really at home for the plain reason that they are incompatible with Christian truth. The more glaring examples are no problem; it is the borderline cases that puzzle us.

Here, as in so many things, Scripture has the answer. For the New Testament gives us a principle* which, if courageously applied, will serve as

* It is because it is a book that gives principles rather than

a criterion for the kind of education that honors God not only in the classroom but also in every part of its program. We find this principle stated by the Apostle Paul in his letter to the Colossians: 'Whatsoever you do in word or deed, do all in the name of the Lord Jesus, giving thanks to God and the Father by him.' [1] For those who are committed to what is good, the criterion is both clear and broad. There is nothing hidebound about Paul's words; everything wholesome, everything happy, everything truly recreative is within their scope. They rule out only those things that cannot be pursued to the glory of Christ and with thanksgiving to God. The test is searching; only activities that are true and worthy can pass it. As for the matter of application, backgrounds and customs enter in. What may be done on one campus to the glory of God may not be allowable on another campus. Christian conscience does not always lead to identical decisions; but when obeyed, it always results in action acceptable to God.

Now assuming that activities compatible with St. Paul's criterion are approved, what of their

lists of 'borderline' practices that the Bible never wears out. To be sure, it speaks in no uncertain tones against downright sins, but in respect to doubtful questions, things that are permissible in one time or place and not sanctioned in another, it sets down no rigid rules but rather gives abiding principles. The fourteenth chapter of Romans well illustrates this point.

union with God's all-embracing truth? The answer lies in a simple fact — work well done, even as a hobby or recreation, effort expended unselfishly, activity that contributes to a life of effective service of God and fellowman — these belong to God's truth fully as much as the most carefully planned course in philosophy or Bible. The reason for this goes back to the apostle's words in Colossians, which bear repetition at this point: 'Whatsoever you do in word or in deed, do all in the name of the Lord Jesus, giving thanks to God and the Father by Him.' That statement is a standard, because it points to the way in which a thing is done. From it we derive the very important principle that the Christian significance of what we do is determined not just by the thing itself; it depends also on the manner of its doing. The rule, in short, is one of method — doing 'all in the name of the Lord Jesus, giving thanks to God and the Father by Him.' * The test, as we have already seen, imposes limitations, because not everything can be done in this way. Funda-

* This criterion of method is far removed from the rootless self-expression of the pragmatism that underlies a good deal of present-day educational philosophy. There is a big difference between the instrumentalism of John Dewey which repudiates supernatural religion, and the Biblical criterion of method which depends on the doing of supernatural and revealed truth.

mentally, however, it concerns the 'how' rather than the 'what' of an activity.

From the foregoing we see that Christian integration relates to more than subject matter; it is a question of method as well. Thus we have what might be called the criterion of craftsmanship, using the term in its broad sense of doing a job well. The teacher who gives himself to his work in real dedication, the student who is not content merely to get by but goes beyond what is required — these, provided their motive reaches past self-advancement to the glory of God, are practicing the principle of Christian craftsmanship. And the essence of this principle is that of the Parable of the Talents [2] in which our Lord praises the use rather than the amount of the individual's enduement.

The rule has its clear application to extracurricular activities. Take, for example, athletics. From the point of view of Christian doctrine, a mile race is in itself a neutral thing. The way in which a young man runs it, however, is so far from neutral that St. Paul did not hesitate to use the Greek games as a powerful figure of the Christian life.

In these days of the overemphasis of competitive sports, almost any mention of athletics raises a question that cannot be evaded. Let us call it the problem of balance or proportion, and let us face it squarely. Some plain speaking is in order. Whenever football, basketball, or any other game holds the full center of attention in a school or college, no amount of talk about Christian sportsmanship, or any resort to prayer before games, can alter the fact that the balance has been upset and integration marred. In the light of this fact the suggestion, recently reported in one of the evangelical papers, that 'Christian bowl games' be organized, takes on a serious aspect. God forbid the carrying out of such a project, which could only mean a tragic lowering of standards! The temptation to be like the Philistines is ever with Christian education, and in few places is it stronger than in relation to the athletic program.

Necessary as the warning is, it must not lead to another extreme — namely, the position that athletics have little place in Christian education, because they are so prone to abuse. The opposite is true. The place of athletics, though always subsidiary to the main business of school or college, is a vital one. It is once more a question of method; especially in sports, the manner in which they are conducted is all important. Teamplay, the heart of which is self-restraint and self-sacrifice; the moral courage that is good sportsmanship — these can be learned on playing fields in such a way that they become lasting character traits to the glory of God. And the benefit of athletics under Christian leadership is by no means confined to participants; the whole school community may learn group lessons in encouraging the defeated, being generous to rivals, and showing under all circumstances the courtesy that is such an essential by-product of the Gospel.

3. Discipline — the Acid Test

We now take a further step away from the classroom and enter the administrative offices. If in the management of any school or college integrity is essential, as it surely is, this sacred obligation is doubly important in Christian education. Few things can be more damaging to students and faculty than a gap between the professed principles and the actual practices of those who are in authority over them. Let us keep this fact in mind as we look at three different administrative responsibilities — discipline, the planning of religious services, and the matter of promotion or advertising.

In many ways, the acid test of a Christian school or college is its handling of discipline. The manner in which an erring student is dealt with speaks volumes about the one who deals with him. Here the center of integration shifts to fundamentals such as love, justice, and responsibility — 'and the greatest of these is love.' It stands to reason, therefore, that the person who exercises disciplinary authority must himself be well acquainted with the love of Christ. His primary motivation should be nothing less than the new commandment: 'That you love one another as I have loved you.' [3] With Paul he must be convinced that 'love never fails.' [4] Everything considered, these are the most important of all words in relation to discipline. The problem is more than a rational one, it goes deep into the emotions. Every discerning teacher is conscious of the fact that the long-continued tension of this violent age is affecting youth. In particular, those of us whose experience goes back as far as twenty or thirty years observe an increase of emotional problems among young people. Although faith remains the greatest source of inner stability, it is unrealistic to assume that Christian young people are immune to the emotional problems of our time. But sympathetic as we are with the problems of youth, sentimentality has no place in their solution. Along with a compassion for the individual and his needs, there must at times be the fortitude to deal severely with the individual in view of that responsibility for the group which is the ever-present burden of educational authority. For the administration of discipline involves the integration of moral truth with outward act.

This is not the time to discuss particular techniques, which are almost as varied as are the different schools and colleges. Far more important than these is the spirit behind them. In a very special sense, the words, 'The letter killeth but the spirit giveth life,' [5] apply to discipline. Here, above all, professional knowledge must be supplemented and directed by the Spirit of God. And it must be freely available. Every student is important. Though a principal or a dean may be too busy to see a teacher, he must never be too busy to see a student. A genuinely Christian handling of discipline is a costly thing; it cannot be achieved without the expenditure of precious hours. The brusque interview and the routine infliction of penalty may seem efficient, but except in very minor matters, they are usually sub-Christian. Patient understanding, the willingness to talk a situation out, above all, the time to pray about it — these are essential to the administration of discipline in Christian integrity. The result will sometimes be action of a drastic kind, but even then Christian love will do its restoring and healing work.

4. Integration Applies to the Chapel Also

Our attention now shifts to religious services. At first thought any inquiry into this field looks like carrying coals to Newcastle. In point of fact, however, it is possible for a school or college to have chapel services of soundest orthodoxy that are yet far from integrated with its Christian purpose. One way to guard against this is to avoid having the majority of services conducted by the same person, whether president, principal, or chaplain. It is much better to bring every faculty member into the chapel program together with some representative students. But this, of course, is possible only in the school committed to the principle of no Christian education without Christian teachers. In a school like this an entire faculty — the teachers of mathematics, English, chemistry, Latin, history, and the other subjects — all taking part in chapel services, may well make an impression for God never to be forgotten.

With an awareness of treading on delicate ground, we turn from the regular chapel service to the special meeting — an aspect of the religious program that needs careful thought. Consider the evangelistic or revival meeting in Christian education today. It is not the need for evangelism that is in question. Apart from the clear presentation of the Gospel of Christ for individual decision, there is no such thing as Christian education. No amount of spiritual nurture can ever obscure the fact that the student who is a stranger to the Lord Jesus Christ is lost and needs to be born again. At the same time, evangelism, important though it is, is not the whole of Christian education any more than it is the sum total of Christian worship.

The problem is this. Every Christian school or college of any size has, spiritually speaking, a student body of mixed nature. Even if regeneration is made a requirement for entrance, there is no way of being sure that all who claim regeneration are really in Christ through living faith. A school can no more claim to have a student body that is wholly Christian than a church can be absolutely certain that every one of its members is truly in Christ. Now in most evangelical schools and colleges many of the students are genuinely Christian; they know whom they have believed and are really committed to Him. Others, however, are not Christian at all. It is they who constitute the chief evangelistic challenge of the institution; without question they must be faced with the necessity of receiving Christ as their Saviour and Lord.

So far the issue is clear. But return to the former group, the students who are already Christians. Look at them again and you will find among them some who, while unquestionably children of God, know neither the day nor the hour of their conversion. Brought up in thoroughly Christian homes, they cannot remember the time of a definite experience of the new birth.

Yet that they are believers is undeniable. They have spiritual life; they are trusting Christ and Him alone for their salvation; they love the Word of God, and they love the brethren also. Generally, however, our evangelism takes little if any notice of them. Instead, the implication is that, because they cannot point to the day or the hour of a particular experience, they have never been saved. So these young people who are truly among Christ's little ones may be led to question, if not even to repudiate, the work of God in their hearts.

The problem needs prayerful consideration. The public invitation for the reception of Christ should take it into account. This invitation might include an opportunity to receive assurance of salvation by claiming the atoning work of Christ as the only ground of acceptance with God. It might encourage those who have never done so to go on record openly regarding their possession of the eternal life that is already theirs. Whatever method is used, one thing is certain: Never should even so good a thing as coming forward in a meeting, or anything that man does, be confused with regeneration. As President Chafer so clearly showed in his book, *True Evangelism*,[6] regeneration is only and always the mighty work of the Spirit of God within the heart. Outward acts are but the evidence of what has been accomplished in the believer through the finished work of Christ.

Years ago Dr. G. Campbell Morgan said publicly that by no means every Christian can remember the time when he was born again. After the meeting, someone challenged his statement. The great English expositor looked at him and said: 'Are you alive?' 'Why, of course, I am,' his questioner answered. 'But,' Dr. Morgan went on, 'do you remember when you were born?' And on being answered in the negative, he asked: 'Then how do you know you are alive?' 'Because I am living now,' was the reply. 'Exactly,' said Dr. Morgan. 'Some Christians may not remember the moment of their new birth. But they are spiritually alive and know it, and that is what counts.' [7]

Perhaps we need in our Christian schools and colleges to make clear the fact that the first proof of the new birth is the possession of eternal life. Let us not hesitate to call for a definite, once-and-for-all decision. Let us leave no student in the false security of a supposed regeneration, when the reality as evidenced by love for Christ and His Word, trust in His saving work, love for the brethren, and the witness of the indwelling Spirit is lacking. But let us always remember that the Bible never requires of believers identity of spiritual experience. Therefore, we have no right ever to set up demands that go beyond the great

principle stated by the Lord Jesus, when He said
to Nicodemus in one of the most important and
beautiful verses in the New Testament: 'The
wind bloweth where it listeth, and thou hearest
the sound thereof, but canst not tell whence it
cometh and whither it goeth; so is every one that
is born of the spirit.' [8] If the workings of the
Spirit of God in the human heart are as various
as the blowing of the wind, we must be careful
not even by implication to confine Him to some
special kind of outward response in fashion in
the meetings of our day.

This is a time when God is graciously using
mass methods of evangelism for the salvation of
many. But a kind of presentation that is effective
with multitudes may not always be best in a
school where the Bible is regularly taught and
the Gospel constantly preached. In such a setting,
conversion is by no means limited to special
meetings. The challenge to decision is always
present. If special meetings are held, their
most effective results are often the quiet, face-
to-face talks that occur when students, having
been touched by the truth in Christ, voluntarily
come for individual counsel.

5. *The Promotion of Christian Education*

To turn from these matters of the spirit to a
subject such as the promotion of Christian educa-

tion through advertising may seem like stepping out of church into the market place. Nevertheless, there is a responsibility for truth in advertising fully as much as in teaching. The field of promotion is one in which the spirit of the age influences Christian education in a subtle way. Publicity in America, though big business, does not always bear the hallmark of truth. Cleverness, catchiness, appeals to pride and snobbery are all features of present-day advertising. Though truth may be paid lip service in the avoidance of overt factual error, it is too frequently violated through deliberate creation of false impressions. Such methods are productive; they get results. But Christian education has no right to follow them.

The temptation is far greater than it was twenty years ago. In the last few decades a whole new school of Christian journalism, heavily supported by advertising, has arisen. Moreover, competition in Christian education has increased. Enrollments have doubled, trebled, and in some cases quadrupled. As a result, it is all too easy to vie with other schools in buying large space and then filling it with striking copy. The various promotional devices, including catalogues and other printed matter as well as magazine advertising, are, of course, not intrinsically wrong. They become wrong when anything of untruth invades their presentation of the claims of Christian education.

The subject is a painful one. No one who has not struggled with the preparation of educational advertising knows how difficult it is to be at the same time truthful and effective. It is so easy to look through rose-colored spectacles at a beloved work and to shade the truth for the sake of effect. Especially is this the case in certain aspects of education in which a good many Christian schools and colleges have been, until recently at least, among the 'have nots.' The reference is to academic standards. We rejoice at the great progress made in the scholastic standing of evangelical education during even the last decades. But to claim that standards are now the highest in the country or faculties the most capable is simply not true. The claim may, if cleverly presented in large spreads with plenty of crowd appeal, increase enrollment. But it is hard to see how the proclamation in classroom and chapel of the Word of God with its tremendous insistence upon truth in every sphere of life can be reconciled with the publication of such advertising.

Let us make a judgment of charity. Without doubt it is a worthy thing to encourage young people to attend schools and colleges that are loyal to the faith. And not only are the motives good; there is surely no conscious effort to deceive. But minimize it as we may, even irresponsibility in handling the truth is a serious fault. One of the chief marks of scholarship is respect for accuracy. The institution that publicizes its own attainments through statements that are themselves inaccurate proclaims that it has yet to learn what scholarship is. The kindest thing that can be said of the advertising pages of some Christian journals is that they present a picture of education which is immature.

Severe as this criticism has been, there is behind it much confidence in the men and women who are responsible for evangelical education in America today. Theirs is too often the task of making bricks without straw. Their burdens are great. But in their hearts they do value truth, and there is no doubt of the fact that, when they realize that the devious methods of some forms of worldly advertising have crept into their presentation of the claims of Christian education, voluntary reform will follow.

6. *The Christian Public*

From administration to the Christian public — this is the last step in our study. Now it is the institution as a whole — the word suggests not just a single school or college but the entire enterprise of Christian education — that is to be examined in relation to its supporters. For it must never be forgotten that all education is a reflection of its environment. The climate of opinion in which it is carried on is bound to influence its policy and practice. So we turn an appraising eye upon what, for want of a better term, we shall call 'the Christian public.' What does it think of Christian education? What does it expect of it? And to what extent are these thoughts and expectations influencing the evangelical school and college, to say nothing of the Bible institute and the theological seminary?

Even a concise attempt to answer these questions should prove fruitful. As we make this attempt, we must recognize certain facts. We live in a time when the opposition to serious thought is great. Superficiality, bred of a hasty civilization so busy manipulating gadgets that it has little time for culture, is a characteristic of our times. Television, comic strips, the pablum of tabloid newspapers and picture magazines — these are not conducive to hard thinking. In an age the watchword of which is 'streamlined,' there is decreasing appreciation of things that really stretch the mind.

It is perfectly plain that the Christian public has not escaped this trend. One of the symptoms of its conformity to the spirit of the age is in its attitude toward education. Yes, it supports Christian schools and colleges, but it supports them out of an attitude that as yet shows comparatively little understanding of the value of sound learning. Some believing parents consider the Christian elementary or secondary school a mere frill or extra, because of the dominance of the public school; and, if the truth be told, others think of it as a sort of educational rescue mission for budding juvenile delinquents and for children who appear to be stupid. For parents like these, Christian education means higher education only. Such a view ignores the plain fact that, if we want our children to have a God-centered world view, the foundations must be laid in early youth.

Lacking appreciation for the broad strategy of Christian education, our public is more taken with its outward manifestations than with its main business. It is to be hoped that the day will never come when our schools and colleges cease sending out Gospel teams, chapel choirs, student preachers, and summer quartets. Participation in youth rallies and other public Christian occasions is important. Yet these are not in themselves the main business of an educational institution. That business is, and always will be, nothing less than to develop sound learning to the glory of God. For young people education is preparation for life-service, which means doing God's will. Preparation itself is work, and the student who to the glory of God does first-rate work in English or mathematics serves the Lord just as much as the student who indulges so fully in outside Christian activities that he lacks time to do his work in physics, or even in Bible. To speak bluntly, too many evangelicals manifest a contentment with intellectual mediocrity, and this attitude is reflected in the young people who come to Christian schools and colleges. Says Dr. A. W. Tozer of *The Alliance Weekly:* 'There is, unfortunately, a feeling in some quarters today that there is something innately wrong about learning, and that to be spiritual one must also be stupid. This tacit philosophy has given us in the last half century a new cult within the confines of orthodoxy; I call it the Cult of Ignorance. It equates learning with unbelief and spirituality with ignorance, and, according to it, never the twain shall meet. This is reflected in a wretchedly inferior religious literature, a slap-happy type of religious meeting, and a grade of Christian song so low as to be positively embarrassing.' [9]

7. The Call for Christian Scholarship

This indictment is not unjustified. And it comes, let it not be forgotten, from one of us. We need in our education a great deal more of the spirit of Sir Richard Livingstone, whose writings [10] plead so eloquently for the primacy of the excellent. In speaking like this, one runs the risk of being branded a cold intellectual without the warmth of the spirit. But learning and intellectuality, as church history abundantly shows, go hand in hand. Take for example Samuel Rutherford of seventeenth-century Scotland, the author of the famous *Letters*. Rutherford was one of the most learned men of his time. His theological treatises are the work of a great scholar. Yet there shines through his magnificent *Letters* a depth of devotion to Christ to which our own superficial age is almost a complete stranger.

'But,' there are those who tell us, 'Peter and John were "unlearned and ignorant men." ' So they were, and God by His grace mightily used them. There was, however, another apostle who, instead of being 'unlearned and ignorant,' was one of the finest scholars of his age. And the influence of Paul, the greatest of all missionaries and the most intellectual of inspired writers, outruns them all. Nor is Paul the only instance of God's use of consecrated intellect. Augustine, Luther, Calvin, Edwards, Wesley — all were men of high education who loved learning and used their minds until their work was done. Study the great turning points of Christian history, and in every case you will find behind them solid learning used to the glory of God. With all due honor to Moody and Spurgeon, who lacked formal education but who valued it so highly that they both founded schools, we must acknowledge that Christian history has in the main been made by men of the highest intellectual attainment.

This fact points to the meaning and purpose of Christian education in our own day. It is not a mass movement and never will be. Now as always its *raison d'être* is the training of Christian leadership in the whole wide realm of God's truth. The reproach of Christ is one thing, and evangelicalism will always have to bear it; the reproach of obscurantism is another thing, and evangelicalism must make up its mind to stop bearing it. The call today is for a renaissance of evangelical scholarship. That renaissance is already under way abroad. In England the evangelical faith has a hold upon some of the best minds in Oxford and Cambridge, to say nothing of fine intellects in lesser institutions. The same is true on the Continent. Books that for scholarship are second to none are being written by earnest Christians. There are also signs that the renaissance is beginning in this country. From the faculties of evangelical colleges and seminaries are coming books and articles of solid worth. Our scholars are making their influence felt in meetings of the great learned societies.

It is true that, as Bible-believing Christians, we look for the coming of the Lord. But by the same token we know that He may delay His coming far beyond our time. We have, then, the obligation to occupy until He comes. To do this we need leadership that is both consecrated and intellectual, and that is integrated both in mind and spirit with the truth of God in Scripture, in nature, in science, literature, art, and in all of life. This is a main function of our Christian education. Christian teaching and scholarship go together. They are indispensable, if the evangelical faith is to reach the present generation.

Let us stop being on the defensive. Ours is a view of Scripture, of theology, and of life that is in the mainstream of Christian history. It demands not apology but bold presentation. Our task is not only to outlive and outserve those who do not stand for God's truth; it is also by God's grace to outthink them.

8. The Challenge of Christian Education

What, finally, shall we say of Christian teaching as a vocation? We must say that it is hard work. It has, like all other worth-while endeavor, its drudgery. It is physically and mentally wearing, as well as stimulating, to deal day after day with immature minds. And it is also nervously taxing. Every true teacher understands in a humble way something of what St. Luke said of the Master Teacher: 'There went virtue out of him.' [11] The financial rewards are not great in any kind of teaching; in Christian education they are still very small. Above all, teaching is not for those who do not like youth — and not every earnest Christian does like youth.

But for those who are called, for those who have for youth a Christ-like love and sympathy, Christian education is a glorious work. It means dealing with the most important and precious material in the world — growing human souls. Few professions bear so plainly the marks of the Lord Jesus, which are the marks of self-sacrifice. The teacher's greatest reward comes not in his own advancement but in seeing his pupils achieve under God far more than he alone could ever hope to achieve. For those whom God calls to serve in it, Christian education is a field wide open. There is pioneer work to be done, especially on the elementary and secondary levels. Within the next decades, scores, if not hundreds, of Christian schools will be founded. New Christian colleges, seminaries, and Bible institutes are yet to be built. As we see the opportunity and its greatness, we are humbled. Like the apostle we can only ask, 'Who is sufficient for these things?' [12] And with him also we can know beyond a shadow of a doubt that, as we are committed to the service of Christ in education, 'Our sufficiency is of God.' [13]

Notes

1. Colossians 3:17.
2. Matthew 25:14–30.
3. John 13:34.
4. I Corinthians 13:8.
5. II Corinthians 3:6.
6. *True Evangelism*, by Lewis Sperry Chafer, Chicago, 1911.
7. One of Doctor Campbell Morgan's sons, Dr. Howard Moody Morgan, pastor of the Chambers-Wylie Presbyterian Church of Philadelphia, recently told the writer that this frequently quoted conversation took place in his hearing after his father had spoken in his church in Lexington, Kentucky.
8. John 3:8.
9. Cf. article entitled 'Moses' in *His*, May 1952. Used by permission.
10. *On Education*, by Sir Richard Livingstone, New York, 1945.
11. Luke 6:19.
12. II Corinthians 2:16.
13. II Corinthians 3:5.

Where, Then, Are Christian Youth To Go?

Whenever the problems of Christian education are seriously discussed, especially in relation to the secularism of our day, one question in particular is always raised. 'Because the secular world view is so pervasive,' someone asks, 'are we therefore to conclude that our young people are to go only to Christian institutions? Is the secular or, to put it more specifically, the non-evangelical school or college never to be considered for any of them?'

To answer the question we need to look for a moment at the state of Christian education in America today. Doing so, we see that evangelical Christian education is top-heavy. It is like an inverted pyramid, resting upon its smallest point. In both number of institutions and number of students its greatest strength is at the top. For many years the lion's share of support has gone to the colleges, Bible institutes, and theological seminaries. But the foundation upon which this superstructure rests has been neglected.

It is not the need for Christian higher institutions that is in question; it is the failure to see the crucial role of the earlier years that has brought the imbalance. The psychology of child development tells us that the early years are the most critical of all. It is then that character and emotional patterns are formed; it is then that the foundations of a Christian world view are laid.

In actual fact, however, only a small minority of Protestant youth are receiving elementary and secondary education with a genuinely Christian integration. The vast majority are in public schools, where a consistent Christian world view cannot be imparted, however good the emphasis upon conduct and character may be. To be sure, in some cases a strongly Christian home and a church with a vital educational program may supply the lack; yet the tide of secularism in America has risen so high that it is difficult to give children in their impressionable years a thorough-going Christian view of life. For youth in the latter position the Christian college has a contribution to make and it will continue to make it with increasing effectiveness, as it becomes more thoroughly integrated with the pattern of God's truth. Practically speaking, it is a case of better late than never. Better give youth a Christian world view in college than not at all, even though for some, college may be almost too late. What has just been said relates to only one function of the private Christian college, an institution that plays an essential part in American education. In proportion to size, it has sent out more leaders than almost any other type of college. Its place is secure and its support well deserved.

But there are others among our young people
whose position is different from that of boys and
girls who reach college age without a really Christian view of the world. There are those who have
been blessed with training in home and church
that has from the beginning given them, in germ
at least, a coherent Christian outlook on knowledge and life. In addition, there are others who
have had the advantage of attending the comparatively few schools where such a view is central. Still others — and included among them
are some from secular homes — have, by the
grace of God working through special agencies of
youth evangelism, had their eyes opened to a
truly Christ-centered view of life. Taken all together, the number of such young people is not
inconsiderable. Some, though not all, may for
various reasons go to the more secular colleges.
If they do, their path may not be easy; they will
face thorny problems and the reality of their faith
will be tested. But if, being thoroughly established in the truth, they are tough-minded
enough to hold fast their Christian orientation,
they will be the stronger for the experience. Not
only that, but some from among them will come
out peculiarly fitted to give evangelicalism the
kind of scholarly leadership it so urgently needs.
What God could do through an Augustine,
trained in the pagan schools of fourth-century
Rome, He can do again in our age.

INDEX